STANDOUT CVs

YOU'RE HIRED! GUIDES

Find Work at 50+
Graduate Career Handbook
Interview Answers
Job Hunting Online
Psychometric Tests
Total Job Search

See **www.trotman.co.uk** for a comprehensive list of published and forthcoming Trotman titles.

YOU'RE HIRED!

STANDOUT CVs

Corinne Mills

trotman | t

To Jonathan, Elliot and Louis
Thank you for your love and patience.

You're Hired! Standout CVs

This third edition published in 2023 by Trotman, an imprint of Trotman Indigo Publishing Ltd, 21d Charles Street, Bath BA1 1HX

© Trotman Indigo Publishing 2023

Author Corinne Mills

British Library Cataloguing in Publication Data
A catalogue record for this book is available from the British Library

ISBN 978 1 912943 86 9

All rights reserved. No part of this publication may be reproduced, stored in a retrieval system or transmitted in any form or by any means, electronic and mechanical, photocopying, recording or otherwise without prior permission of Trotman Indigo Publishing.

Every effort has been made to trace copyright holders and to obtain their permission for the use of copyright material. The publisher apologises for any errors or omissions and would be grateful to be notified of any corrections that should be incorporated in future editions of this book.

Printed in the UK by Severn, Gloucester

All details in this book were correct at the time of going to press. To keep up to date with all the latest news and updates and to access the online resources that accompany this book, use this QR code or visit **indigo.careers/standout_CVs**.

CONTENTS

List of activities	ix
About the author	x
Introduction	1
Part One Researching you	**3**
Chapter 1 Gathering the facts	7
Fact not fiction	8
Contact details	8
Career background	10
Professional qualifications and memberships	11
Education	12
Knowledge	13
Training and development	15
Additional information	16
Beware of oversharing	17
Chapter 2 Prove yourself	23
Your skills and strengths	24
How competent are you?	25
Using AI to help you	26
Aptitude testing	30
Chapter 3 Highlighting your achievements	33
Value added: why employers like achievers	34
Dutiful or high achiever?	35
So, what have you achieved?	35
Writing your achievement statements	37
Chapter 4 So, what are you really like?	41
What every employer wants	42
What are you like?	43
Personality testing or 'testing' personality?	45

CONTENTS

Part Two Match-making	47
Chapter 5 Show you are the perfect fit	51
Decoding job advertisements	52
Job descriptions and person specification forms	55
How do you rate?	57
Researching an organisation	59
Researching the employer's market	62
Part Three Devising your CV	67
Chapter 6 Choice language	71
Speaking volumes	72
Me, myself and I	72
The magic of words	74
Pitch perfect	78
Technical words	78
Keyword search	79
Chapter 7 The first half page of your CV	83
Your CV headings	84
Personal information	84
Writing a career profile	86
Writing a career objective statement	91
Chapter 8 Chronological CVs	95
Template for a chronological CV	97
Chapter 9 Functional CVs	103
Template for a functional CV	106
Chapter 10 One-page CVs	113
Template for a one-page CV	116
Chapter 11 Developing your own CV website	119
How to create your own website	120
What to include on your website	121
A consultancy service's website	122

Chapter 12 Making your CV look good	125
Making your CV look attractive	126
Say 'cheese!'	128
Quality control	128
Chapter 13 CVs for specific career challenges	131
CVs for graduates and school-leavers	132
CVs for career changers	139
CVs for people with career gaps	143
Technical CVs	148
Creative CVs	153
CV advice for managers and executives	157
CVs for internal promotions	161
Part Four Using your CV	**165**
Chapter 14 Building an online CV	169
Building an online CV for job websites	170
Job notifications	172
Chapter 15 Sending your CV by email	175
Format compatibility	176
Email etiquette	176
Writing a covering email for your CV	177
Chapter 16 Social media profiles	183
What is social media?	184
LinkedIn	184
YouTube	188
Blogs, podcasts, webinars	188
Your digital reputation	189
Chapter 17 Job-search strategies	191
Advertised jobs	192
Networking	195
Speculative approaches	196
Recruitment agencies	197
Headhunters	198

Part Five Additional resources **201**

Chapter 18 Other resources 203
Other people 204
Free career support services 204
Commercial services 205

Chapter 19 And finally... 211

LIST OF ACTIVITIES

As you read this book, you will see the [download] symbol, which indicates that there is an online resource to help you with this section. All these activities are available online at **indigo.careers/standout_CVs**, where they can be downloaded ⬇ and used to help you create your standout CV.

1 Information gathering	21
2 Identifying your strengths and skills	24
3 Your competency examples	31
4 Identifying your achievements	36
5 Writing your achievement statements	40
6 Your personality and preferences	44
7 Your market research	64
8 Keyword selection	80
9 Writing a career profile	92
10 Your CV checklist	162

ABOUT THE AUTHOR

Corinne Mills is the Managing Director of Personal Career Management (**www.personalcareermanagement.com**), the UK's leading career coaching and outplacement company. It has been described as the 'best in the business' by many of the UK's leading recruitment players. Corinne and her team of specialist career coaches help individuals to be happy and successful in their career. This includes helping people understand their work personality, and how to create a working life that plays to their strengths and needs. Corinne's team also advises on all aspects of career management, including personal branding and how to land that coveted job.

Corinne has worked for 30 years in the career management field, helping thousands of individuals with a wide array of career challenges. They have ranged from senior executives – including FTSE 100 CEOs – and entrepreneurs, aspiring leaders and experts in their field, to career changers and those at the start of their career.

Prior to working in career management, Corinne was an actress and sometime singer in a New Wave band, before changing career to work in HR, where she was responsible for hiring, performance managing and, occasionally, firing people. She is a Fellow of the Chartered Institute of Personnel and Development, with an MA in Human Resource Management.

Her first book, *You're Hired! CV: How to write a brilliant CV* has consistently been the UK's bestselling CV book since publication, proving highly popular with both the general public and industry experts. Corinne's hugely successful second book *Career Coach* (Trotman), is for those who are at a career crossroads and unsure about their next career move.

Corinne, who's been called 'the career guru' by the BBC appears regularly on BBC TV and radio, ITV, Channel 4 and Sky News as well as writing for many national newspapers.

INTRODUCTION

CV writing looks like it should be easy to do. However, anyone who has tried it knows that it is not as straightforward as it seems. This is because your CV has to work on many different levels. On the one hand, it is a straightforward historical record of your skills, qualifications and employment history. While on the other, it's the cornerstone of your personal branding – how you represent yourself to others professionally. It needs to set out a carefully crafted business pitch of your usefulness and why people should want to meet with you and hire you.

It is deceptively tricky.

The chances are that you are reading this book because you have realised this, either because you are writing your CV for the first time, updating your old one or because your existing one isn't having the impact you want.

The aim of this book is to help you create a standout CV that gets you noticed, shortlisted for the roles you want, and positively warms up the interview panel before you get in the room. It's also going to show you the fundamentals of how to talk persuasively about yourself professionally, which will be helpful in all aspects of your career, from interviews and networking, to talking to your boss.

The book, firstly, helps you gather the information you need, then shows you how to structure and finesse the content of your CV to impress both human recruiters and technological candidate tracking systems. You'll also learn how to use the latest AI (Artificial Intelligence) technology to your advantage.

Accompanying this book are online tools (available at **indigo.careers/standout_CVs**) featuring helpful activities and checklists. Look for the ↓ symbol, which indicates that there is an activity on the website for you to complete. All the activities are downloadable, so you will have all the information readily available whenever you need it.

The great thing about your investment in this book and the time and energy you spend on working through it, is that there is a direct return. A standout CV is time efficient, increases your earning potential and job satisfaction, improves your employability, and opens up options for the future. Well worth it!

Happy job-hunting!

Corinne Mills
www.personalcareermanagement.com

PART ONE

RESEARCHING YOU

CHAPTER 1
Gathering the facts

CHAPTER 2
Prove yourself

CHAPTER 3
Highlighting your achievements

CHAPTER 4
So, what are you really like?

Talking to strangers?

Before any employer will take you on, they will want to know about you in detail. Part One of this book is going to help you prepare the factual information that you need to present in your CV, as well as identifying the skills, abilities and personal qualities that will help you get shortlisted.

When you see ⬇ symbol, you can visit **indigo.careers/standout_CVs** for activities that will help you capture all the information you need. You can download them to your own computer for easy access.

By the end of Part One, you will have completed the first, key building block in assembling your CV.

1 GATHERING THE FACTS

At its most simple level, your CV is a historical record of who you are, what you have done and your contact details. The first step in writing a new CV, or even revising an old one, is to ensure that the facts are complete, accurate and appropriate. This chapter is going to help you gather together and check that you have all of the factual information about yourself that is needed.

This chapter will help you:

- identify the essential information you need to include on your CV
- ensure authenticity and accuracy
- avoid oversharing to your disadvantage.

Fact not fiction

Every CV should include the following factual information:

- name and full contact details
- details of your career history
- professional qualifications and/or professional memberships
- educational record
- relevant skills and knowledge
- relevant training and development.

Although this seems very straightforward, getting it wrong, as candidates frequently do, can have serious implications. Factual information that has been supplied by a candidate and which is found to be false, may not only exclude you from any other applications to that organisation, you could even be subject to criminal proceedings if you are found to have obtained a role through deception.

So let's go through each of the items in the list above to make sure there are no omissions or gaffes.

Contact details

Name
Decide the name you want to be referred to and stick to this throughout. In your private life, people may call you something slightly different, e.g. Kate if your name is Catherine, but try to ensure that professionally you refer to yourself in a consistent way to avoid any confusion. If you have a fairly common name, e.g. Jane Smith, then you may wish to add an initial or middle name to your CV to differentiate yourself.

Location details
Rather than supplying your full address, you need only include location details so that employers know where you are based, e.g. Manchester M1 1AG, even if it's for a remote role. Recruiters will often use location criteria to filter candidate lists where a local candidate is preferred.

It's no longer recommended that you include full address details on your CV, especially when it's posted on a recruitment site, because of the risks of identity theft.

Telephone contact number

Recruiters will need your mobile phone number to contact you, so make sure that you have recorded a professional sounding voicemail in case you're not available when they call. Recruiters will be making assumptions about you and your professionalism by the way you handle your messaging, and you don't want to put them off before they've even spoken to you. Don't rely on the default factory setting version as this won't say who you are, and the recruiter may not leave a message if they are unsure it's you.

Email address

Use a personal email address for your job-searching activities rather than a current work email address where someone else might have access to your emails. It's worth setting up a new email address specifically for job searching and applications. You can always close it down later if you no longer need it or if it becomes a magnet for spam. You can easily create a new free account from gmail, outlook or other mailbox services.

Make sure that your email address is suitably professional. Your surname with initials or numbers usually works best. However, avoid using 'O' or 'I' unless they are part of a recognisable word. This is because it can be difficult for email senders to distinguish between the letters 'O' or 'I' and the numbers 'zero' or 'one', respectively. For example, Olivia222@hotmail.com is clear, whereas OliviaIII@hotmail.com makes it difficult to see whether the 'I' is a capital 'i' or a lower case 'L' or the number '1'.

Don't use family email addresses, e.g. themacallisters@gmail.com, as employers want to contact *you* – not the whole household. And be aware that jokey emails, such as jonathan@sexanddrugs.com, are unlikely to play well with recruiters, even if it makes your friends laugh.

Career background

Employers want the factual details of your work history, qualifications and other credentials. Listed below is the information you will need to produce and it's suggested that you read this through, then at the end of this chapter you'll see the ⬇ symbol and link to **indigo.careers/standout_CVs**, where you can gather all your own information.

Career history

- **Previous employers:** list all your previous employers, with some additional information about their size, turnover, key products or services. You can usually find this information on their website. Later, you can use this information to draw the recruiter's attention to any similarities between your previous organisation and the one you are applying to, e.g. related products or similar size.
- **Dates of employment:** these must be accurate as employers will check these against references and your LinkedIn profile. If you've an employment gap, you can record the dates as month to month, e.g. January 2022–November 2023, or even 2021–2023, rather than the precise dates.
- **Key duties and responsibilities:** for each role, include some brief bullet points about what you looked after and the key duties you performed. Focus on how you actually spent your time rather than what your job description said, because these can often be quite different. You may find the prompts listed in the box below helpful. Wherever possible try to quantify your answers with numbers, e.g. responsible for five major customer accounts.

> **PROMPTS FOR THINKING ABOUT YOUR WORK EXPERIENCE**
>
> - Why did your role matter, and how did it help the organisation?
> - What were you able to achieve that you are proud of? What were your successes?
> - Who were your customers? How did you work with them?
> - What technology systems or other equipment did you use?
> - Who did you communicate with, and how? E.g. producing reports for management, providing feedback to clinical staff or quality assessors.

- Did you have any people responsibilities? E.g. recruiting, training, mentoring or managing staff. If so, how many?
- Were there any financial responsibilities? E.g. budget management, keeping costs low, generating revenue.
- Did you work on any projects? If so, what did you do and what were the aims and were there any positive outcomes?
- How did you help reduce organisational risks? E.g. ensuring compliance on standards, spotting errors, technical updating.

Professional qualifications and memberships

Vocational qualifications and/or professional memberships

List any qualifications you have achieved that are industry related or recognised by professional associations. These could include certificates, diplomas, BTECs, NVQs, apprenticeships, degrees or postgraduate training, e.g. a certificate in health and safety or a PGCE (postgraduate certificate in education).

Professional memberships

List your memberships of any professional organisations, e.g. the Chartered Institute of Personnel and Development, as this shows your commitment to certain professional standards and to updating your expertise.

> *Membership of a professional association gives you career credibility, showing you have met required standards and are conscientious about updating your skills and knowledge. Many also offer fantastic resources in terms of a job board, networking opportunities and other career resources.*
>
> Michael Schwoerke, Global Employability Lead at ACCA (Association of Chartered Certified Accountants)

Education

University or college education

Write down details of any degree or college courses for which you have studied. Note the grade achieved, the dates of study and the name of the institution. Where you have more than one degree, list them all, with the most recent or the most relevant first.

Secondary school education

Capture the qualifications you attained at school and your dates of study. Normally, you'll only need this information if you have less than five years' job experience, or perhaps to prove your English and maths skills if you don't have a higher qualification. However, it's also worth including your school education if you had excellent A level grades but a disappointing university result. If you do this, then be prepared to talk at interview about why your degree results were poor by comparison. The employer may have sympathy for mitigating circumstances, but not for partying too hard.

If you are a first-time job-seeker, you should also make a note of other school activities in which you were involved to show off your capabilities. Examples include:

- being a school prefect, youth council member or running a student interest group
- engaging in extra-curricular activities in the arts, sports, science or business challenges
- participating in National Citizens Service, the Duke of Edinburgh scheme, Scouts or Guides
- undertaking voluntary work, including helping in the community or for a cause.

MAKING THE GRADE!

If you've ever been tempted to 'improve' your grades on your CV...

- Employers will often check your academic record and may ask you to produce your certificates.

- If you lie and are found out, then any job offer is likely to be withdrawn.
- You can be dismissed at any time in your employment if you are found to have lied at the recruitment stage.
- Even worse, you can be convicted for fraud, even imprisoned, and ordered to repay your salary obtained under false pretences.
- Many successful people did poorly at school or didn't go to university, e.g. Richard Branson.
- As your career progresses, school qualifications become less important with the more work experience you acquire.
- Showing an ongoing willingness to learn is essential. This could be on-the-job training – it doesn't need to mean exams.
- It's never too late to study if you want to. Most courses that require entry level qualifications also have access routes for those without them.

Knowledge

What do you know about that the ordinary person on the street – or even people within your field – might not, e.g.:

- mobile phone contracts
- how to help vulnerable customers
- trade compliance standards
- plant propagation
- managing volunteer teams
- operating precision equipment
- maintenance of home burglar alarm systems
- merchandising for fashion brands
- software programming within the creative industries
- procurement requirements within the National Health Service (NHS).

Information technology (IT) packages
These are so essential that it is worth noting all IT capabilities and your level of ability.

Publications/research/conferences/ industry working groups or panels

This is usually for subject matter experts who are sharing their knowledge or insights more widely than within their organisation.

> *If you want to position yourself as an 'industry expert' or 'thought leader', then refer on your CV to your knowledge of the latest trends and ideally how you've helped influence these – for instance, delivering webinars, writing articles, running research projects, or membership of policy working groups. Post these on your LinkedIn page and provide regular updates.*
>
> Carly Bower, Career Coach

Hobbies/interests

Write down all your hobbies and interests. It is not strictly necessary to include these on your CV, but it can help enliven what might otherwise be a fairly conventional CV. For instance, if you enjoy wild swimming, gaming, writing fiction or following a football team, then it gives an opportunity for some light banter with an interviewer who probably feels – quite rightly – that these reveal a little more about your personality.

Most importantly, if you decide to include a hobby on your CV, then make sure it is genuine and shows you in a good light. Avoid mentioning anything that could be perceived as contentious.

Voluntary work

Think of all the voluntary activities you have been involved in over the past few years. This could include helping others during the Coronavirus pandemic, being part of the PTA at your local school, running a kids' football team, litter picking with a local conservation group, or fundraising for a charity.

Employers are very interested in socially responsible activities. They indicate energy and community spirit, the kind of behaviours they want to see in their own organisations.

Voluntary work can also help bridge perceived gaps in your paid work experience when applying for a new role. For instance, an unpaid role on a committee could extend your knowledge about organisational strategy or governance; working with vulnerable people requires advanced interpersonal skills; or acting as a treasurer requires financial skills; or if you've volunteered as a mentor, then you can show how you've built strong relationships and used your emotional intelligence to good effect.

Voluntary work that is undertaken to help you build specific skills also demonstrates to an employer that you are serious about your next career move, because you have invested unpaid time and energy in order to gain these capabilities.

If you aren't working currently and have a gap since your last job, enrolling for voluntary work at least a few hours a week will be enormously beneficial. It will give you an answer to the interview question: 'So what have you been doing since your last job?', and you will also be using your skills and making contacts.

Training and development

Note any training or development that you have undertaken. This could include any of the following:

- in-house courses, such as customer service
- external courses, such as PRINCE2, or presentation skills
- e-learning packages, such as cyber-security training or programming
- attending conferences or webinars, or reading on particular subjects
- being on the fast-track 'talent pool' at work
- coaching or mentoring, both as a coach or as a coach'ee'
- voluntary work training, such as learning listening skills as a Samaritan
- secondment opportunities, work shadowing or other development opportunities.

Make a note of any courses you are currently undertaking and their estimated completion date. Employers like to see that you are continually learning and updating your skills.

Additional information

Think about whether there is any other personal information that may be of interest to an employer, such as:

- a driving licence
- dual citizenship
- language skills
- significant achievements, such as completing a marathon or winning a prize for your photography
- other roles undertaken, e.g. magistrate, non-executive director.

Nationality/work status

If your background and experience are predominantly from a different country, it is helpful to state your citizenship/work status. If you've full rights to work in the country, then it will reassure employers that you are very easy to hire. If you need sponsorship or there are other conditions attached to offering you employment, then it's best to be upfront about this as you will be asked about it anyway. As eligibility arrangements are subject to change, international candidates need to proactively check their permissions to work.

Referees

You will need two individuals who are happy to act as a referee for you. Ideally, they should be your current and past managers. If this is problematic, then you could ask someone equivalent in seniority within the same organisation or someone with whom you had a key business relationship, e.g. a customer whose account you managed. If you are a first-time job-seeker, you can ask your course tutor to provide a reference.

Always check with your referees that they are happy for their details to be forwarded to prospective employers. Do not assume that they will be happy for this to be done. The last thing you want is a referee who is unhappy with you because you haven't extended them the courtesy of asking them.

> *I had a candidate's referee on the phone who was very reluctant to give a reference for the applicant (who had specifically given me his name and number). When I asked whether the candidate had performed his duties to the company's satisfaction his reply was:*
>
> *'I'm sure there was nothing wrong with his work, but since I found out he's been sleeping with my wife I'm finding it difficult to say anything nice about him.'*
>
> Anon, Human Resources Manager

Although you need to have your referee's details handy, do not include them on your CV. The only exception to this is if they are extremely well known in their field and likely to be well regarded by the recruiter, in which case definitely show off your connections.

Why is it important to retain control of your referees? If your current manager is a referee and they are not yet aware that you are looking for a new role, you need to make sure that you are going to be offered the job before you hand over your manager's contact details. It also gives you an opportunity to brief your referees on the job you are applying for and what you think the prospective employer would like to know about you. You can then remind them of all the wonderful things you did for them that demonstrate how you meet the employer's requirements. This is especially helpful if you are going for a different type of job and need your referee to be 'on message' regarding your transferable skills.

If the employer says they want referees at the start of the recruitment process, say that you are happy to supply references after your interview. Most job offers are made subject to references, so it's not usually a problem, and handling it this way means that you can use your referees to best advantage.

Beware of oversharing

Date of birth
In the UK and many other countries, it is unlawful to discriminate against candidates because of their age. Employers must consider your suitability in

terms of your skills and experience, not how young or how old you are, which means it is no longer necessary to include your date of birth on your CV.

However, it is usually possible to determine roughly a person's age because of the dates of their qualifications and experience. So, omitting your date of birth is not a foolproof method of avoiding direct or indirect age discrimination.

If this is something you are concerned about, you can choose to omit any work experience or background from more than 20 years ago unless directly relevant to the role in question. If you are relatively early in your career, then the dates of your academic qualifications are going to put into context why you haven't got much work experience yet.

Marital/family status
There is no requirement to include your marital status, number of children or other dependants – and little value in doing so.

Religion, political affiliations, sexuality and gender
While this is a matter of personal choice, it's generally recommended that you do not share information on religion, political affiliations, sexuality or gender on your CV, unless they are specifically relevant to the role in question; for instance, if this shows how you share certain values or experiences central to the mission of the organisation. You can include your pronouns, but it is not a requirement.

If any of these areas could have an impact on how you would do the job – for instance, any accommodations for religious reasons – then it is far better to talk with the employer about this once you have been offered the job, rather than on your CV.

Disabilities
You don't need to disclose a disability or periods of ill health on your CV. The aim of your CV is to focus on what you can do, rather than any limitations. However, if you will need some adjustments for your interview or any assessments, then it is sensible to request these ahead of time. Employers are generally very responsive to this, not only because they are legally required to make reasonable adjustments, but because many want to be more inclusive.

> *Under the Equality Act 2010, a person is disabled if they have a physical or mental impairment that has a substantial and long-term negative effect on their ability to do normal daily activities. There are some conditions, such as cancer or multiple sclerosis, which are automatically considered to be disabilities under the Equality Act. If you are disabled under the Equality Act, you are protected from discrimination not only when you get the job, but also as a job applicant.*
>
> Jessica Bass, Partner at Oury Clark Solicitors

Reasons for leaving

Some application forms ask for reasons for leaving an organisation. **This is not required on a CV – so don't volunteer it.**

It is essential that you make no direct or implicit criticisms of previous employers on your CV. Undoubtedly, there will have been jobs you enjoyed more than others, and some which were not enjoyable at all. You may have been made redundant, had a difficult relationship with a manager or colleague, or simply been bored by the job. However, employers want to hire candidates who have had good and positive relationships with previous employers. So make sure that your CV does not contain any hints of grievances, personality clashes, or complaints, no matter how justified you are.

Some online application forms will insist that you declare your reasons for leaving. In this case, choose a positive reason like 'seeking career development' or 'organisational restructuring', which suggests your exit was part of a bigger organisational strategy rather than a decision about you personally.

Criminal convictions

You do not need to disclose that you have a criminal record if you are not asked to do so. However, if a recruiter or employer does ask, then there are some circumstances when you have to declare it, and others where you do not, depending on whether your conviction is 'spent' or the special nature of the role and organisation. You can find useful guidance on this at **www.gov.uk/tell-employer-or-college-about-criminal-record/check-your-conviction-caution**.

If you have to declare a conviction, then this is best done via a separate email or conversation so that you can provide some context and reassure them that you will be an excellent employee. **Do not mention any criminal convictions on your CV**, as this should be a wholly positive document focusing on why you are a great candidate for the job.

According to Dominic Headley, a leading expert on criminal records, Government policy has been to try and improve employment outcomes of people with convictions. This has included the creation of a dedicated department called the New Futures Network (**www.newfuturesnetwork.gov.uk**), which helps serving prisoners and prison leavers into jobs. As a result, many organisations are now proactively recruiting people with convictions to fill their skills gaps or to fulfil their social value obligations within their government contracts.

You can find useful resources on all aspects of ex-offenders looking for work by contacting the charities Nacro (**www.nacro.org.uk**) or Unlock (**www.unlock.org.uk**) and you will also find many useful resources on Dominic Headley's own website **www.dominicheadleyassociates.co.uk**.

Caring responsibilities

There is no need to state that you have caring responsibilities on your CV. If you do, you might raise a query in the employer's mind about your non-work commitments and availability. Far better to apply for roles likely to give you the flexibility you need, and mention your caring responsibilities after you've been offered the job (if you feel you need to).

There is legislation in place to help employees who need time off for dependants, and flexible working is so much more commonplace that there is no value in raising this as a potential issue when it may not be one.

ACTIVITY 1: INFORMATION GATHERING

Let's gather together all the factual information you will need to create your CV, as outlined in this chapter and the CV Checklist below. ↓ At **indigo.careers/standout_CVs** you can capture your answers in an online form, which you can then download to your own computer. It will then be ready for you to copy and paste into your CV document or applications, whenever you need it.

TABLE 1: CV CHECKLIST

	Include ✓ / Don't include ✗
Name	✓
Location	✓
Mobile no.	✓
Personal email address	✓
Career history • Dates of employment • Brief description of company • Your role and why it mattered • Your successes	✓
Areas of knowledge and expertise	✓
IT, technology skills and equipment handling	✓
Professional memberships	✓
Training and development	✓ If relevant
Publications, research, policy-making, media experience	✓
Voluntary and community work	✓
Vocational qualifications • Dates, courses and grades	✓
Further and higher education • Dates, courses and grades	✓
Secondary school education • Dates, subjects and grades	✓ Only if less than 5 years' work experience
Extra-curricular activities as a student	✓
Additional information, e.g. language skills	✓ If relevant or impressive
Legal right to work in the country	✓ If from an international background
Hobbies and interests	✗ Unless relevant or interesting
Referees	✗ Supply after interview
Religious or political affiliations	✗ Unless directly relevant to the organisation

21

Sexuality, gender	✗ Pronouns optional
Disability, illness	✗ Do not put on CV, but you can disclose on company's own diversity monitoring forms or via covering email if needed
Criminal convictions	✗ Do not volunteer this on CV; there will be a separate process to follow if disclosure is required
Date of birth, marital status, number of children, caring responsibilities	✗
Reasons for leaving, any conflicts with employers, etc.	✗

IN A NUTSHELL

This chapter has focused on ensuring that the factual information that you should include in your CV is complete, correct and appropriate. Remember to:

- make sure all the information on your CV is accurate

- ensure all of your contact details are fully functioning and businesslike

- make sure that sensitive issues, such as disability, criminal convictions, etc., are dealt with separately from the CV

- keep all your factual information easily accessible, because you will be referring to it frequently.

2 PROVE YOURSELF

You may know that you are the best person for the job. You may feel 100% confident that your prospective employer will never find anyone as skilled as you to do the job. However, the employer doesn't know that. You have to prove it to them! This chapter looks at how you can give the employer the evidence they need that you have the skills they are looking for.

This chapter will help you:

- identify your personal skills and strengths

- understand competencies and how they are used by employers

- use AI to generate examples that help you prove your key skills and competencies

- discover the ways that employers can test your aptitude and ability.

Your skills and strengths

Most people can describe what they do in their job, but find it less easy to identify their personal skills and strengths. It's important to be able to articulate what you are good at if you want prospective employers to understand the contribution you can make to their organisation.

> **ACTIVITY 2**
>
> ## IDENTIFYING YOUR STRENGTHS AND SKILLS
>
> Your strengths are usually on display when you are involved in a work activity that you enjoy, when you are so immersed that you don't notice the time passing. This tends to be when you are using your natural abilities. For instance, you might like helping others or solving problems.
>
> Your skills are usually learnt and developed, rather than innate. For instance, you may have learnt sales technique, but your natural resilience has also helped make you a successful salesperson.
>
> Let's look at your skills. Consider the following questions to help you discover your strengths and skills – and don't be modest!
>
> ↓ This activity is available at **indigo.careers/standout_CVs** for you to download and save. You'll also find there a list of skills and strengths that you can choose from to help identify your capabilities.
>
> 1. What do you think are your natural strengths? What do you enjoy doing at work, and what comes easily to you?
> 2. What skills have you acquired (i.e. what are you good at that you have learned how to do)? This may include some skills you really enjoy using, as well as others that you are capable of but less enthusiastic about.
> 3. What do other people think are your strengths and skills? If you're not sure, ask them. Gather feedback from people at work whom you trust, and review past performance evaluations. Also ask family and friends. People will see you from different perspectives, but their insights can often illuminate things you have missed.

How competent are you?

Now that you have thought about what you are good at, let's look at what employers want. 'Competencies' (also known as 'competences') refer to skills, expertise and behaviours that an organisation feels are required for an individual to perform effectively in a particular role.

There will be specific competencies required for different roles, depending on the context and your level of seniority. These may include specific technical competencies around subject matter expertise, technology and practical experience. However, to some extent, the following general professional competencies are core to every role, as they are what make you an effective employee.

TABLE 2: KEY COMPETENCIES

Competency	Characteristics
Communication skills	Clarity, listening, influencing, verbal and written skills
Social intelligence	Adept in working with different people and in varied situations
Customer focus	Winning customers and nurturing customer relationships
Results orientated	Goal focused and getting things done
Agile learner	Able to learn quickly, adaptable and flexible
Commercial savviness	Able to improve performance, profits and cost-effectiveness
Team working	Supportive, collaborative, inclusive when working with others
Change maker	Identifies ways to improve things and makes change happen
Self-management	Organised, motivated and an effective planner
Critical thinking	Analysing, logical problem solving, using judgement
Creativity	Offering fresh perspectives and ideas
Resilience	Performing under pressure and meeting challenges
Digital literacy	Understanding and using digital systems

Employers will use competencies like these as criteria for shortlisting candidates by:

- seeing if you can provide good examples of when you have demonstrated these competencies
- giving you case studies or theoretical examples, and asking you to outline your approach to the challenge set
- asking you to perform tasks or activities designed to test those competencies, e.g. at online assessments or observing you in the task.

Unless you provide good examples in your CV giving evidence of these types of competencies, you may not get the chance to prove them at interview. So, how can you go about this?

Which of the following two statements do you think is the more credible and why?

- I am good at handling conflict.
- Working in events, I have become very adept in managing conflict. This includes calming down difficult guests by actively listening to their complaints, problem-solving wherever possible and, if needed, arranging for their removal from the premises.

The second sentence paints the picture of how a particular skill has been demonstrated, and this is the key to providing the proof that an employer is looking for in your CV; and this is where AI tools can prove very useful.

Using AI to help you

The new Artificial Intelligence language models can be incredibly helpful with CVs and job applications, especially if you are stuck for ideas, or need help in finding the right words or structure to express your thoughts.

Many of them are also free to use. Whichever one you are using – for instance, ChatGPT; Microsoft's new Chat feature, which is now integrated with Bing and their Edge web browser; or Google's Bard – they all work along similar lines. They use a chat function and, by asking questions or prompts, their answers can help you research, generate and write useful content on most topics in a way that will be clearly expressed and grammatically correct.

This can be especially helpful when it comes to writing your CV. However, it is essential that any content you use in this way is both checked for accuracy, as AI does make mistakes, and that it is also personalised. Your CV has to authentically represent you and your own real life experience; otherwise, even if your CV is nicely written, it will be superficial – and that's not going to get you anywhere.

> **HOW TO ACCESS AI**
>
> You can access AI for free on your computer, tablet or mobile phone. There are lots of options being rolled out as the technology develops. Try the following routes. (NB: Some are still at the experimental stage, but are no less useful.)
>
> - www.bing.com (look for the Chat function)
> - www.chat.openai.com
> - www.bard.google.com
> - Microsoft Co-pilot, which will work across Microsoft products.

Let's look at how you might use AI to aid your thinking about your skills and how you might express these in your CV.

For this example we're going to use the free Microsoft Bing web browser at www.bing.com. You'll need the function marked 'Chat'. If you don't already have it on your system, you'll need to grant your PC access to Microsoft Edge; if you are an Apple user, try the ChatGPT version that is being developed.

Let's assume you are looking for a role as a project co-ordinator, and you feel you have a fairly good idea what is required but you want to double-check this. Here are the prompts you might use.

> You: *Hey Bing. What type of competencies and skills are required to be a project co-ordinator?*
>
> Bing: *Some of the most common competencies and skills required for a project coordinator are:*

● *Communication skills: You need to be able to communicate clearly and professionally with different people and groups involved in the project, such as team members, stakeholders, clients, vendors and media outlets. You also need to be able to convey information, instructions, feedback and reports in various formats, such as oral, written and visual.*

● *Organisational skills: You need to be able to manage multiple tasks, resources and deadlines in a structured and orderly manner. You also need to be able to prioritise, delegate and monitor the progress and performance of the project activities and deliverables. You also need to be able to document, store and retrieve information and data efficiently and accurately.*

● *Problem-solving skills: You need to be able to identify, analyse and resolve problems that may arise during the project. You also need to be able to anticipate potential risks and mitigate them before they become problems. You also need to be able to use logical and creative thinking, brainstorm and evaluate solutions, and learn from your mistakes and successes.*

● *Leadership skills: You need to be able to lead and motivate the project team and stakeholders. You also need to be able to foster collaboration, cooperation and trust among the project participants. You also need to be able to set clear goals, expectations and standards for the project. You also need to be able to provide feedback, recognition and support .*

● *Budgeting skills: You need to be able to create and manage the project budget. You also need to be able to track and control the project expenses and revenues. You also need to be able to identify and implement ways to reduce costs and increase profits. You also need to be able to report on the financial performance of the project.*

Bing's answer is drawn from its own synthesis of information available on the web, and while I haven't listed them here, the answer it gave also provided useful references and websites to find out further information.

This answer is useful because it gives more detail about what each competency means, whereas often in the person specifications for jobs they only give single words or phrases, such as 'problem-solving skills'. Bing may also flag up additional competencies it thinks will be required which may not be in the person specification but are likely to be equally important.

Next, you can refine this further by taking one of the competencies.

> You: *Hey Bing! Give me three great examples of how I could demonstrate that I've got problem-solving skills on my CV when I am applying for a role as a project co-ordinator?* [If Bing's response is a bit long and vague, then it often helps to ask: *Bing, Can you make this more concise?*]
>
> Bing:
> - *Resolved technical issues and stakeholder conflicts in a software development project, delivering it on time, within budget and with high quality.*
> - *Implemented creative solutions to attract donors and supporters for a fundraising event, managing the logistics and budget, and addressing any challenges or risks, raising £10,000 for the cause.*
> - *Conducted market research and analysis, developed and executed a digital marketing strategy, monitored and measured the campaign performance, and made adjustments as needed, increasing the product awareness and sales by 50% and 30% respectively in the first quarter.*

As a project co-ordinator, you may not quite have done any of these, but Bing has come up with some useful ideas you can pursue, for instance:

- *Were there any technical issues you did help resolve? If so, what did you do and what difference did it make?*
- *What creative ideas did you have, perhaps when helping organise an event?*
- *What research and analysis have you done? What did it help with and what was the impact?*

Bing's answer also gives you a useful structure for the type of content you could use: stating the challenge, what you did, and some measurement of its impact and reach. However, you must personalise it from your own experience, providing examples that you could genuinely talk about at interview. For instance, if you had worked on a project for a new learning platform, you could ask Bing to help you write about it as follows:

You: *Hey Bing, as project co-ordinator I worked on a new learning platform that had a lot of problems, which I helped resolve. How can I write about this to show my problem-solving skills for a project manager role?*

Bing: *Used problem-solving skills to resolve various issues with a new learning platform, such as technical glitches, user complaints, and training gaps. Worked with the IT team, the users, and the trainers to identify, analyse, and implement solutions. Improved the user experience, satisfaction, and performance of the learning platform.*

You can then refine this further by adding in some detail about the kinds of glitches, the solutions you helped broker and how the improvements were measured, e.g. user feedback measures or a reduction in IT help desk calls.

You can do this with each of the competencies you think are required for the jobs you are interested in, as well as the more general professional competencies outlined in Actiovity 3 (opposite). If the answers get too long, then just ask Bing to be more concise.

Aptitude testing

Many employers and recruitment websites ask candidates to perform tests that help verify whether they actually have the competencies they claim. This might be a verbal or numerical reasoning test, a personality questionnaire or a work-related task — either at the application stage or later in the process. The accessibility of AI to candidates, and the ease with which anyone can write a convincing CV, will mean that candidates are likely to face more testing in the future and more probing interviews in order to assess how genuine their CV is. This makes it even more important that your competencies are authentic and that you can back them up with evidence.

ACTIVITY 3: YOUR COMPETENCY EXAMPLES

Let's look at how you can prove you have the competencies outlined earlier. ↓ You can complete this activity at **indigo.careers/standout_CVs** and download your answers.

Key competencies

- Communication skills
- Social intelligence
- Customer focus
- Results orientated
- Agile learner
- Commercial savviness
- Team working
- Change maker
- Self-management
- Critical thinking
- Creativity
- Resilience
- Digital literacy

1. For each of the key competencies listed above, think of real-life examples that demonstrate you showing this competency. There is an explanation of each competency in Table 2 (see page 25). For instance, you could show your ability to be creative by talking about your redesign of a document, problem-solving a solution to a tricky issue, or your introduction of imaginative use of visuals to communicate an idea.
2. Provide some data to back up your example; such as, the number of people you helped, the size of the project, the £s earned or saved, the % increase in productivity, time saved or cost-effectiveness.
3. Experiment with AI to help you with ideas, but ensure that your examples are genuine and rooted in your real-life experience so you are able to talk about each example in depth at an interview if you are asked to do so.

IN A NUTSHELL

In order to write your CV you need to have a clear, objective view of the skills and competencies you are offering to an employer and what they require. This chapter has helped you:

- identify your key skills and strengths
- understand the competencies that an employer will be looking for
- discover how to use AI to research required competencies and how to write content that will prove you have these
- understand that employers may also set ability tests, so any claims you make on your CV regarding your abilities must be realistic.

3 HIGHLIGHTING YOUR ACHIEVEMENTS

Chapter 2 was about proving your strengths and skills to the employer. Using achievement statements in your CV is a way to show that you can use those skills, not just for their own sake, but to deliver meaningful results for the organisation. It shows employers they are likely to get a return on their investment if they hire you.

This chapter will help you:

- understand why employers like achievements on CVs

- identify the achievements you have made

- write achievement statements for your CV

- record your achievements in an easily usable form.

Value added: why employers like achievers

Many candidates write their CVs like a job description. They faithfully list the duties they performed and their responsibilities. However, they fail to show the positive impact of their work on the team or organisation as a whole.

The whole point of employing someone is that they can make a contribution to the organisation. Employers are interested in employing staff who can:

- solve a problem for them
- increase profits and/or reduce costs
- sell more and/or open up opportunities
- improve efficiency and/or quality
- generate ideas and/or enable positive change
- enhance customer satisfaction and/or staff productivity.

If the employer can see that the salary they will be paying you will be more than offset by your contribution to the organisation's effectiveness, then it makes the hiring decision easier for them.

> *Including a track record of your achievements in your CV makes you a much more desirable candidate for an employer. They'll figure that if you've been a high performer and made a positive difference in previous organisations, then you're also likely to be able to do the same for them.*
>
> Jane Garrard, Career Coach

Including your achievements in your CV helps to present you as a person who:

- focuses on results and gets things done
- does over and above what is required in the role
- understands the needs of the wider organisation.

3 HIGHLIGHTING YOUR ACHIEVEMENTS

Chapter 2 was about proving your strengths and skills to the employer. Using achievement statements in your CV is a way to show that you can use those skills, not just for their own sake, but to deliver meaningful results for the organisation. It shows employers they are likely to get a return on their investment if they hire you.

This chapter will help you:

- understand why employers like achievements on CVs
- identify the achievements you have made
- write achievement statements for your CV
- record your achievements in an easily usable form.

Value added: why employers like achievers

Many candidates write their CVs like a job description. They faithfully list the duties they performed and their responsibilities. However, they fail to show the positive impact of their work on the team or organisation as a whole.

The whole point of employing someone is that they can make a contribution to the organisation. Employers are interested in employing staff who can:

- solve a problem for them
- increase profits and/or reduce costs
- sell more and/or open up opportunities
- improve efficiency and/or quality
- generate ideas and/or enable positive change
- enhance customer satisfaction and/or staff productivity.

If the employer can see that the salary they will be paying you will be more than offset by your contribution to the organisation's effectiveness, then it makes the hiring decision easier for them.

> *Including a track record of your achievements in your CV makes you a much more desirable candidate for an employer. They'll figure that if you've been a high performer and made a positive difference in previous organisations, then you're also likely to be able to do the same for them.*
>
> Jane Garrard, Career Coach

Including your achievements in your CV helps to present you as a person who:

- focuses on results and gets things done
- does over and above what is required in the role
- understands the needs of the wider organisation.

Dutiful or high achiever?

If you are not convinced whether achievement statements make much difference on a CV, then compare the duty and achievement statements in Table 3 to see which you think are most attractive to any employer.

TABLE 3: DUTY VERSUS ACHIEVEMENT	
Statements indicating 'duty'	**Statements indicating 'achievement'**
Responsible for inducting new staff	Inducted over 20 new staff in departmental procedures to ensure consistency of approach and high-quality customer service
Introduced mentoring scheme	Introduced mentoring scheme to over 30 new staff per year; this improved staff retention and enabled new employees to quickly become effective in their role
Trained staff in Excel	Trained 50 staff in Excel, which increased the capabilities of staff and their time efficiency in producing reports
Purchased new factory equipment	Researched and purchased new factory equipment, which led to a 30% increase in packaging efficiency
Responsibilities include credit control	Since taking over the credit control function over 95% of long-standing debts have been recovered, some of which had been owing for more than 2 years
Responsible for pool maintenance	Reduced leakages by changing sealant, which meant existing liner could be repaired rather than replaced, saving over £5,000 in materials and staff costs

The achievement statements reinforce the impression of the candidate as someone who understands and does their best to support the wider business needs of an organisation rather than an employee who is a 'jobsworth' doing the bare minimum.

So, what have you achieved?

No matter what roles you have been working in or how long your career has been, there will be things that you have achieved that you can use on your CV to create that positive impression. However, this is one of those activities where it is not always easy to be objective about yourself and realise the impact that you have made. So let's look at how to get you thinking about your achievements.

Achievements should be work related: show things you are proud of and which have had a positive impact for your team or organisation. If your role is an outcome-related one, e.g. sales and marketing or projects, then focus on results in terms of increased sales, value of contracts won, or project milestones successfully delivered. For charitable or non-commercial roles, choose examples where you helped meet the organisation's aims, whether by helping it to be better able to serve its community or by improving how it operates.

You might find it helpful to look through previous staff appraisal records as a reminder of your performance objectives and what you achieved.

ACTIVITY 4

IDENTIFYING YOUR ACHIEVEMENTS

↓ This form is available at **indigo.careers/standout_CVs**, where you can complete your answers and download it for your reference.

1 Think about the following questions to help you gather your achievements and the contribution you have made at work.

- What positive feedback have you received at work and why?
- Have you received any awards, commendations or nominations?
- What personal, team or organisational targets have you met?
- How did you save time, money or resources for the organisation?
- Have you helped increase profits, customers and sales?
- Did you help improve quality or increase efficiency at work?
- Did you improve customer service for internal or external customers?
- What work challenges have you faced that you were able to overcome?
- What have you helped to change, and what has been the impact?
- Have you helped make a positive impact in the wider world?

2 ↓ Go to **indigo.careers/standout_CVs** to capture your answers.

Writing your achievement statements

Now you need to think about how you are going to write this information in a way that you can use on your CV. Here are some guidelines to help you.

There is the well-used **STAR** formula, which describes the **S**ituation, the **T**ask involved, the **A**ction you took and the **R**esult. This can work well at an interview, but can be a bit wordy on a CV; so, you can also use this formula.

Beneficial result　　+　　what you did that made this happen

Example: Saved management time and improved customer experience [beneficial result] by introducing an effective complaints escalation procedure [what you did].

or

What you did　　+　　beneficial result

Example: Introduced complaints escalation procedure [what you did] which saved management time and improved customer experience [beneficial result].

- The statements should be between one and three sentences long.
- Use positive words, see pages 74–77 for ideas.
- Include some detail (but be succinct) about what you did and how you did it.
- State the difference that was made to the work/team/organisation as a result of this achievement. Quantify this with numbers, percentages if possible, or using estimates if you don't have exact numbers.
- Ensure these are things that you can justify happened as a result of your contribution, rather than being a more general achievement of the team or organisation.
- Be prepared to talk about these achievements in detail at an interview.

On the following page are examples of Achievement Statements for two different roles to give you some ideas.

ADMINISTRATOR – SOME ACHIEVEMENTS

- Revitalised our 50-page operations manual, updating it, simplifying processes and introducing helpful video content and links. It's now far easier and quicker to train staff.
- Improved client experience by changing the online contact forms. Queries are now routed and resolved more efficiently, reducing waiting times by an estimated 10%.
- Commended by the CEO for my activities as an internal well-being champion, helping run quarterly meet-ups and being an ally for three colleagues appreciative of support.
- Quickly learnt the new in-house software and, as a result, was asked to train 12 colleagues from other departments who were finding it challenging.
- Received excellent feedback from a business event I organised for 20 people. Attendees loved the thoughtful but low-cost touches I introduced, like personalised welcome packs.

MARKETING MANAGER – SOME ACHIEVEMENTS

- Delivered an additional £500,000 profit per annum as a result of launching a 'Refer a Friend' scheme, offering fun rewards to those introducing new customers.
- Created a new social media campaign to raise awareness, which has already reached 5 million views, with positive responses from key influencers, celebrities and politicians.
- Won the 'Best Marketing Campaign' award at a national conference for the way in which we used diverse client stories to successfully engage different audiences.
- Identified market trend for customer personalisation and worked with design team to create a new offering positioning us as a front-runner in this £1 billion market.
- Achieved a brand re-launch within four months from inception, including a complete redesign of packaging and promotional materials. The product is already delivering a 10% increase in revenue.

Table 4 lists some prompts to help get you started.

TABLE 4: PROMPTS FOR ACHIEVEMENT STATEMENTS

Won contract for…	Eliminated errors by…
Increased average weekly sales by…	Won award for…
Widened market share by…	Learnt new… which…
Reduced costs by…	Devised new system which…
Graduated within the top 1%…	Tackled issue of… by… as a result…
Improved customer ratings by…	Implemented new… which…
Built relationships which…	Promoted because of my work on…
Advised on… which…	Developed new policy which…
Motivated underperforming team by…	Reorganised… which resulted in…

Using AI to help you

You can also use your AI chat buddy to help you with identifying your achievements using the following prompts.

- *Hey Bing. Give me five examples of achievements I could talk about when writing my CV for a job as…*
- *Hey Bing. I'm proud of having achieved… What is the best way to talk about this on my CV?*
- *Hey Bing. My job involves responsibility for… How can I write this as an achievement statement for my CV?*

Here's an example.

You: *Hey Bing. I'm responsible for security, but how could I write about this as an achievement statement on my CV?*
Bing: *Here are some examples of how you could write about this:*
- *Developed and implemented a comprehensive security plan that reduced theft by ?%.*
- *Conducted regular security audits and made recommendations that resulted in a ?% reduction in security incidents.*
- *Trained and managed a team of ? security personnel to ensure the safety of all employees and visitors.*

- *Received recognition from senior management for maintaining a safe and secure work environment.*

Remember that everything on your CV needs to be authentic and personalised, including your achievements.

ACTIVITY 5

WRITING YOUR ACHIEVEMENT STATEMENTS

1. Review your answers from Activity 4 and your AI research.
2. Write at least six achievement statements that you can use on your CV.
3. Each achievement should include the following information:
   a. The problem, challenge or opportunity
   b. How you tackled it
   c. Quantify this with numbers, % or other data to help demonstrate the impact made. Give a realistic estimate if you are not sure.
4. ↓ Go to **indigo.careers/standout_CVs** to capture your answers.
5. Download and save this content as you will need it later.

IN A NUTSHELL

This chapter has focused on highlighting your achievements on your CV. You should now:

- understand how achievements can create a positive impression on a CV
- be able to write at least six achievement statements that you can include in your CV
- be able to talk about your achievements in depth at an interview.

Table 4 lists some prompts to help get you started.

TABLE 4: PROMPTS FOR ACHIEVEMENT STATEMENTS

Won contract for...	Eliminated errors by...
Increased average weekly sales by...	Won award for...
Widened market share by...	Learnt new... which...
Reduced costs by...	Devised new system which...
Graduated within the top 1%...	Tackled issue of... by... as a result...
Improved customer ratings by...	Implemented new... which...
Built relationships which...	Promoted because of my work on...
Advised on... which...	Developed new policy which...
Motivated underperforming team by...	Reorganised... which resulted in...

Using AI to help you

You can also use your AI chat buddy to help you with identifying your achievements using the following prompts.

- *Hey Bing. Give me five examples of achievements I could talk about when writing my CV for a job as...*
- *Hey Bing. I'm proud of having achieved... What is the best way to talk about this on my CV?*
- *Hey Bing. My job involves responsibility for... How can I write this as an achievement statement for my CV?*

Here's an example.

> You: *Hey Bing. I'm responsible for security, but how could I write about this as an achievement statement on my CV?*
> Bing: *Here are some examples of how you could write about this:*
> - *Developed and implemented a comprehensive security plan that reduced theft by ?%.*
> - *Conducted regular security audits and made recommendations that resulted in a ?% reduction in security incidents.*
> - *Trained and managed a team of ? security personnel to ensure the safety of all employees and visitors.*

- *Received recognition from senior management for maintaining a safe and secure work environment.*

Remember that everything on your CV needs to be authentic and personalised, including your achievements.

ACTIVITY 5

WRITING YOUR ACHIEVEMENT STATEMENTS

1. Review your answers from Activity 4 and your AI research.
2. Write at least six achievement statements that you can use on your CV.
3. Each achievement should include the following information:
   a. The problem, challenge or opportunity
   b. How you tackled it
   c. Quantify this with numbers, % or other data to help demonstrate the impact made. Give a realistic estimate if you are not sure.
4. ↓ Go to **indigo.careers/standout_CVs** to capture your answers.
5. Download and save this content as you will need it later.

IN A NUTSHELL

This chapter has focused on highlighting your achievements on your CV. You should now:

- understand how achievements can create a positive impression on a CV
- be able to write at least six achievement statements that you can include in your CV
- be able to talk about your achievements in depth at an interview.

4 SO, WHAT ARE YOU REALLY LIKE?

Skills and experience are not the only things being judged on your CV. Whether you like it or not, the employer is making a judgement about the kind of person they think you are. This chapter looks at how your CV needs to take personality factors into consideration, by helping you:

- understand why employers are interested in your personality

- identify your own personality and work-style preferences

- provide examples for your CV that show the employer that you have the 'desirable' personality traits they are looking for.

Employers invest much time and money in recruiting new staff, so they are understandably keen to get a return on that investment. They want staff who can not only do the job, but are also motivated and get on with the other people they are working with. Most of us have had experience of working with someone who is difficult, and know the negative impact they can have. Employers are right to be cautious about whom they let into their organisation. If you can reassure them on your CV that you are an asset, not a liability, then you make yourself far more employable.

What every employer wants

Below are some of the personal traits and behaviours that every employer looks for in a candidate. They may not explicitly state that they are looking for these, but they will be looking for clues in your CV, and in your whole approach to your job search, that this is you.

WANTED...

- Can-do attitude
- Positive energy and enthusiasm
- Openness to learning
- Confidential
- Honest
- Represents the company well
- Adaptable to change
- Manages own emotions
- Sensitive to the needs of others
- Resilient
- Conscientious
- Ethical
- Hard-working
- Reliable

How do you convince them that this is you? Talk on your CV about the following:

- demanding deadlines reached and targets achieved
- additional tasks you have taken on over and above your core role
- high trust responsibilities, e.g. dealing with confidential matters
- your compliance with ethical codes or regulations
- recent learning you have undertaken
- your versatility in working with different people

- where you have represented the company externally
- challenges that tested your resilience but where you achieved what was needed
- positive working relationships you have built or poor ones that you have repaired
- how you have supported others
- conflict situations you have resolved.

> *A key point to remember in tailoring your CV is to make sure you communicate a sense of who you are and how you work best. To do this, seek to understand your work style, values and what motivates you at work. This means you can target organisations where you are likely to work well.*
>
> Janet Sheath, Career Consultant

Also be mindful that the way your CV is presented, along with its covering email, needs to echo the professional personality you are trying to convey. It needs to be impeccable in its layout, with no errors, and delivered within any deadlines set.

What are you like?

Regardless of what employers want, as individuals we also have our own unique style, preferences and behaviours. Some of these you will be aware of, others may be more unconscious. Your CV is likely to exhibit some of both kinds of characteristics, either overtly – for instance, in the kinds of achievements you choose to include – or subconsciously – perhaps in your use of particular words or how you present your CV. Candidates tend to use much more positive language to describe the things they enjoy, and more functional language around everything else.

It is helpful to do some self-research on this. You can then identify and make a feature in your CV of some of the particular personality characteristics you have that will be of positive advantage in the role. You can also check (and get someone else to double-check) that you're not inadvertently creating the wrong impression.

Activity 6 will start you thinking about some of your key personality traits and preferences. As with Activity 2 on Strengths and Skills, it is difficult to be objective about yourself, so it is worth asking other people how they view you and seeing if their answers match your own self-perception. Ask them to highlight what they think your personality strengths and behaviours are – and the things you need to watch out for.

ACTIVITY 6

YOUR PERSONALITY AND PREFERENCES

Think about the following questions and also ask others for their feedback. There are no right or wrong answers, so don't answer how you would like to be seen or as if you are at a job interview. Instead, think of how the questions relate to how you really are and your actual work-related experiences.

⬇ This form is available at **indigo.careers/standout_CVs**, where you can complete your answers and download it for your reference.

- How would you describe your workplace personality? What are the consistent features, and have you noted differences in particular roles?
- How would other people at work describe you? (Ask them, look at appraisals and other feedback you have received.)
- What role(s) do you often find yourself taking in group situations? For example, leader, facilitator, creative, facts and figures person, listener, technical expert, practical, advisor, learner, thinker, challenger, mediator, analyst, relationship nurturer, organiser, disruptor, big picture or detail person?
- Do you feel energised by new people, places and experiences, or can this feel draining? Where are your limits?
- Which do you enjoy working with the most: facts and figures, abstract concepts, practical things, people or something else? (See Activity 2 for your strengths.)
- Do you have a structured approach to your work, or are you more spontaneous?
- At work, do you easily express your thoughts and emotions, or do you tend to keep these to yourself?

- Do you feel comfortable handling conflict or challenging others? Have there been some times when you felt more confident in this than others? If so, why was there a difference?
- What causes you stress at work, and what helps you manage it?
- Are you competitive? If so, when does this show itself?
- What do you need to work at your best? For example, input from others, financial reward, change in surroundings, targets and deadlines, thinking time, challenges to solve, opportunities to learn, flexibility, sense of higher purpose.
- How do you respond to successes and mistakes made by yourself or others?

Personality testing or 'testing' personality?

There is a whole industry devoted to helping employers assess whether your psychological profile is the right one for their organisation. Organisations will have researched, or at least made their best guess, about what they think are the common personality characteristics of high performers for particular roles, e.g. competitiveness for salespeople or conscientiousness for those working in quality control. They then test candidates to see if they share those characteristics.

The tests usually ask you to describe yourself or how you would react in certain situations. These can be trickier to answer than you think, as the answer that will help get you shortlisted is not always obvious. Also, if you find yourself answering inauthentically because you think this is what they want to hear, then maybe this isn't the right job for you.

If you are due to take a personality test as part of a forthcoming process, or you simply want to do some more self-research, then some of the test providers provide sample practice tests for you to try. You can also try the excellent free strengths and personality report at **www.marcusbuckingham.com/gift-of-standout**.

While there are lots of free or inexpensive professional and personality tests available online, the usefulness of their reports is variable, and they are usually trying to persuade you to buy their other services. Check out the British Psychological Society website (**www.bps.org.uk**) for useful guidance on psychological testing.

IN A NUTSHELL

This chapter has focused on how your personality is part of the selection criteria for shortlisting and has helped you to:

- understand that employers will often make a judgement about your personality on the basis of your CV alone
- recognise how you can influence employers' perception by using examples within your CV that show your personality in a positive light
- ensure that the image you present is a consistent and genuine one, so that the content and presentation of your CV match the person they will be meeting at the interview.

PART TWO

MATCH-MAKING

CHAPTER 5
Show you are the perfect fit

Selling your services

Part One of this book helped you identify and prove the skills, knowledge and personal qualities that you can offer an employer. However, this is only one side of the story. You need to make sure there is a buyer for what you want to sell. Thousands of candidates apply each year for roles for which they are undoubtedly capable, only to be rejected because they have failed to show in their CV exactly why they are suitable.

Part Two is designed to help you ascertain what the employer is really looking for, rather than relying on assumptions. By the end of this section, you will have brought together all of your research and have in place the key justifications for your CV of why you should be hired for the role.

5 SHOW YOU ARE THE PERFECT FIT

Candidates often make assumptions about what they think a role entails, either because they have read the job details too quickly or because they presume it's similar to others they have experienced.

Knowing how to read job adverts properly and conducting additional research will give you an important competitive advantage.

This chapter will help you:

- decode job adverts and their hidden hints
- use job descriptions and person specifications effectively
- research target organisations and their markets
- research the wider job market for your ideal role
- use all this information to tailor your CV specifically to the employer's requirements.

Recruitment is a matching exercise. The easier it is for the employer to match your CV with their requirements, the greater the likelihood you will be shortlisted. So, let's look first of all at how we can find out what they are looking for.

Decoding job advertisements

The first and most obvious place to look first is at the job advertisements. Let's review a couple of seemingly similar jobs for a legal assistant. Highlight what you think are the main requirements for each job.

ADVERT 1: LEGAL ASSISTANT

An experienced and efficient legal assistant, ideally with experience of working within corporate finance, is urgently required.

Your ability to research, prepare and track legal documentation quickly and accurately is essential, along with strong IT skills and experience of using contract management systems.

Relevant legal qualifications are an advantage.

ADVERT 2: LEGAL ASSISTANT

If you are looking for an exciting role, then this is your perfect opportunity.

You'll be working for two dynamic Partners who specialise in corporate finance. They are often abroad on business, hence they are looking for a superb organiser with excellent interpersonal skills who is comfortable representing the firm to VIP clients.

You'll be helping prepare legal documentation, so will also need strong data management and IT skills.

While there are many similarities, there are important differences too. Let's look closely at the first advert to decode it and how to respond to it.

TABLE 5: ANALYSING ADVERT 1 FOR A LEGAL ASSISTANT

Advertisement	Analysis
An experienced and efficient legal assistant	State how many years' experience you have as a legal assistant and any related qualifications to demonstrate your suitability early in your CV; they want an experienced pair of hands not a novice. 'Efficient' also indicates it is important to convey your speed and accuracy; use phrases in your CV like 'producing documents quickly' or 'achieving fast turnarounds' to indicate that you work at pace.
... experience working within corporate finance	Important to state any experience you have had within this area. If you don't have this, they may not hire you; but it may be possible to convince them if you can show that you've had other roles that are related, e.g. working with a Finance Department or a bank.
... is urgently required	If you can start immediately, say so, as this would be a definite advantage. They may also be flexible on some of their selection criteria if you show you can start quickly.
... Your ability to research, prepare and track documentation quickly and accurately is essential.	Give examples of the type of research you've undertaken, your accurate notetaking, document preparation and information management duties, as these are clearly a huge part of the role. Ensure the spelling and grammar in your CV and covering letter are 100% perfect to show your attention to detail.
Strong IT skills and experience of using contract management systems...	Mention your IT skills early on in your CV profile, especially Word, Excel and any legal or in-house software. If you were involved in contract management, then talk in detail about what you did and the systems you used to manage it. Emphasise how quickly you have learnt new IT systems and your continuous updating to reassure them that it will be easy for you to learn their systems.
Relevant legal qualifications	State your legal qualifications at the top of your CV. If you are studying for them then mention this in your CV profile with an indication of when you will be qualified. If you're not qualified, then they may be persuaded if you tell them you are about to enrol on a relevant course.

The first job advert for a legal assistant focuses on the need for strong information management skills, researching, preparing and tracking information and using the internal IT systems in an efficient and accurate manner. Let's now analyse the second role.

TABLE 6: ANALYSING ADVERT 2 FOR A LEGAL ASSISTANT

Advertisement	Analysis
If you are looking for an exciting role, then this is your perfect opportunity.	This suggests an environment that is fast paced, far from routine and suitable for candidates who like a challenge rather than a quiet life; use positive action words within the CV to show your energy, e.g. 'created', 'averted', 'solved'.
You'll be working for two dynamic Partners who specialise in corporate finance.	The ability to build strong trusted relationships with these Partners is going to be very important; show in your CV how you have had positive working relationships with other managers, e.g. 'Worked closely with my Manager on complex cases, who entrusted me to...' The use of the word 'dynamic' in this context also suggests high energy, a demanding pace and changeable situations; emphasise in your CV how you are used to working in such environments, including any experience in corporate finance.
They are often abroad on business...	Their absence means that they'll want candidates who are self-reliant and need less hand-holding. This may also mean that you are on call outside of normal working hours, especially if you are organising travel, etc. Think of examples for your CV that show your ability to work with minimal supervision and use your initiative, e.g. handling a tricky situation or an out of hours emergency.
...hence they are looking for a superb organiser with excellent interpersonal skills	This role has elements akin to an executive assistant, where you are supporting the Partners with whatever they need to operate successfully. Your CV should show your versatility as a capable organiser, your skills in building and managing relationships, your discretion in handling confidential matters and your experience communicating with different audiences, including clients, other departments and external bodies.
...who is comfortable representing the firm to VIP clients	If possible, name-drop on your CV the name of prestigious companies or individuals. If not, then anonymise them but keep the VIP element by labelling them by their job titles, e.g. CEOs, by the type of company, e.g. a global brand or government department, or by describing them as a 'well-known public figure', 'high net worth individual' or 'celebrity'.

| ...You'll be helping prepare legal documentation, so will also need strong data management and IT skills. | Similar to the first advert, there is also a requirement to have strong IT skills and be familiar with legal information processes; provide full examples of your legal documentation experience and IT skills, including any qualifications. |

While both adverts are seeking candidates with a similar professional background, the first wants someone very strong on data management; the second needs someone who will be more public-facing, representing the partners and organising their diaries. The CV should be focused differently for each one.

Job descriptions and person specification forms

More detailed information on a particular job is often given in a job description and person specification form. These are usually, but not always, made available to candidates before they apply for the post — either the organisation will send it to you or you can access it via its website. It is always worth asking if there is one available for you to look at, because although job descriptions will vary in the amount of detail provided, their aim is to tell you exactly what the employer wants. This makes your task of matching their requirements on your CV much more straightforward.

Recruitment agencies may not always supply this information, either because they don't have it or because they are trying to protect the employer's anonymity or their commission. However, if it's a job you are interested in and you are invited to interview, you should always ask for a job description and a person specification so you can prepare accordingly; you could also send them a new CV ahead of the interview if you think it sells you better.

Job description
This will usually list the job duties, responsibilities and reporting structure for the role. You can see the kind of activities you will be involved in, as well as any people management and financial responsibilities. Organisations will have their own format for their job descriptions and all their recruitment forms, but they will usually look something like the example given on the following page.

SAMPLE JOB DESCRIPTION

Client side developer
Reporting to: Client side manager
Location: Pulham
Staff reports: None

Gladstone Computer Technologies is looking for an experienced, professional and enthusiastic front-end developer to join a world-class team.

Key responsibilities

- To write complex code using HTML, CSS, and JavaScript and other equivalent client side technologies.
- To liaise with the product manager to ensure that all technical possibilities are explored and that products achieve the best possible look, feel and functionality.
- To work with designers and software engineers to ensure that interactive elements of designs work.
- To work with all relevant parties on the deployment of code to the live site.
- To monitor work against the production schedule closely and provide progress updates and report any issues or technical difficulties to the Senior Client Side Developer on a regular basis.

A person specification form (see Table 7, opposite) is usually attached to the job description and it summarises the criteria that the employer will use to determine whether you meet the shortlisting requirements.

TABLE 7: SAMPLE PERSON SPECIFICATION CRITERIA FOR CLIENT SIDE DEVELOPER

	Essential – E Desirable – D
Knowledge	
Knowledge of /HTML, CSS and JavaScript	E
Experience of commercial web development processes	E
Knowledge of information architecture principles and techniques	D
Qualifications and training	
Relevant degree, e.g. in computer science, maths or engineering	D
Appropriate web development qualifications/training	E
Key competencies	
Ability to simplify complex problems or projects, exploring and evaluating them systematically, identifying and resolving problems	E
Ability to present well-reasoned arguments to influence others	E
Able to take initiative with a proactive approach to work	E
Ability to communicate with technical and non-technical audiences	E
High-performance working to demanding deadlines	E

How do you rate?

Most organisations will assess a candidate's CV or online application depending on how well it fulfils each selection criteria for instance:

- 3 points for fully meeting the criteria
- 2 points for partially meeting the criteria
- 0 points for failing to meet the criteria

The scores are likely to be weighted more heavily for essential criteria over desirable criteria.

Many larger companies and *all* job websites will use recruitment software to help recruiters find and rank candidates depending on how well they match the selection criteria. The recruiters are then likely to read only enough of the most highly ranked CVs to create their shortlist for interview. We cover this in more detail in Part Four.

Many good candidates fail to get the high score they deserve and onto the shortlist pile because they make assumptions about what employers will 'read into' a CV.

For instance, you may be an experienced administrator applying for a role where diary management skills are a key requirement. You might figure that because you have been an administrator that the employer will likely know that diary management has been one of your duties. However, administrator roles vary greatly, and if you have not explicitly mentioned diary management in your CV, ideally with a clear example of when you have done this, then neither the recruiter nor the recruitment software algorithms will give you a high score.

So, never assume that employers will just 'know' that you have what they are looking for. Spell it out loud and clear with examples to ensure you are assessed as 'fully meeting the criteria'.

What if I don't meet all of the criteria?

You might feel that you are a very good fit for the role, even if you don't meet all of the criteria. If so, it's still definitely worth an application, but there's no point hoping they won't notice the gaps – they will. You'll need to reassure them it's not an issue if you are to stand any chance – try the following strategies.

- Admit that you don't meet a particular criterion, but list ways in which you could easily bridge the gap: 'Currently teaching myself Sage and, as a quick learner who has learnt several other finance software packages, I'm confident that I'll master it quickly.'
- Use transferable experience: 'Although I have not worked in account management, I have always worked in customer-facing environments where relationship management was essential.'
- Show your motivation and research: 'Although I do not have direct experience of working in advertising, I studied a module on this at college, have attended several webinars with leading practitioners, and have read many books and articles about the industry's challenges and future trends, as this is where I hope to focus my career.'

Researching an organisation

Just like people, organisations tend to have their own personalities or cultures. As we saw in Part One, employers will select candidates who they believe will fit in within their organisation. It is therefore useful to find out as much as you can about how the organisation likes to operate. It gives you the chance to represent yourself as just the kind of person who would thrive in that environment.

If you know anyone who works in your target organisation, or is one of their suppliers, competitors, etc., try to talk with them to find out more about what it is like to work there. Sometimes, organisations give a contact name for you to ring so that you can find out more about the job. Always take up this opportunity, as it enables you to gain a more realistic picture of what the job entails and also to hear exactly what they are looking for in their ideal candidate, which isn't always as clear in the job description. Just remember that this is also a chance to show how interested you are in the job and why you are a good fit, as well as to ask them questions.

Edgar Schein, an eminent organisational psychologist, wrote in his book *Organizational Culture and Leadership* (5th edn, Wiley, 2016) that you could get a sense of an organisation's culture by:

- the way the organisation looked and its visual symbols, e.g. its logo
- how the company talked about itself
- the assumptions and beliefs taken for granted by the people who work there.

Many of these aspects you will unconsciously register when applying to a particular organisation. The way it handles the recruitment process, the information it sends to candidates and its website, all reveal essential information about the company's culture.

The organisation may have a careers page on their website with details of available roles. It might also describe what it's like to work there, although in practice this is sometimes more wishful thinking than reality. This is why it's so important to do further research using the routes suggested on the following page.

Let's start with their website. What does the organisation's website content tell you factually about their:

- origin story, evolution, values and ambitions for the future
- size, locations, any executive or team profiles and their background
- range of products and services and its customers
- standards, and what it works to, e.g. quality, regulatory or best practice
- latest activities, including business and PR news.

Also, looking at the type of words and images the company uses on its website and promotional materials, what impression do you get? For instance do they seem to you...

- down to earth or sophisticated
- a luxury, cool or budget brand
- traditional or innovators
- person-focused or technology-orientated
- formal or relaxed
- altruistic or profit-driven
- creative or functional
- community-orientated or for a niche audience
- proud of their founder, expertise, awards or customer satisfaction.

Those impressions hold important clues, because the organisation is likely to want to recruit in the image it is trying to portray.

But don't stop there! Look at any social media pages they have, particularly LinkedIn, Twitter and Facebook, as they will be posting updates and you'll be able to see dialogue that the organisation is having with other people, including colleagues, customers or the general public. You can pick up lots of very useful information on how the organisation operates in this more informal but still very public space.

Also see if they are mentioned on **www.glassdoor.com**, which is a website where people post their personal views of what it is like to work for an organisation or apply for a job there. While you may discover people with exceptionally good or bad experiences, look for any consistent themes that come through, as these can be very insightful.

How do you use this information for your CV? Table 8 below gives some examples of different types of organisational personality, with advice on how you can tailor your CV to match both the individual job requirements and the wider cultural fit.

TABLE 8: ADAPTING YOUR CV TO SUIT DIFFERENT TYPES OF ORGANISATIONAL CULTURE

Organisational culture	Emphasise in your CV
Altruistic	
Focus on a higher value, i.e. an outcome that is other than monetary gain, e.g. charity organisation	Your strong identification with the organisation's purpose
	How you've helped make a positive impact allied with their mission, e.g. charity or community work
	Your creativity working with a limited budget or resources, as finances are often tight in these organisations
Tightly controlled	
Working in a regulated field, or where public accountability or leadership style is key, e.g. banks, the Civil Service	How you've worked to professional standards, strict policies and processes or performance targets
	Where you've rectified problems where rules weren't observed
	Use words and phrases like, 'diligence', 'attention to detail', 'compliance', 'managing risks', 'monitoring' to show you are a safe pair of hands
Entrepreneurial	
Innovative, risk taking, e.g. big companies like Microsoft or business start-ups	Focus on growth; for instance, how you developed something from scratch, e.g. a process, team, customer base or system
	Show your agility and how your roles have evolved with new responsibilities and technologies
	Use the latest buzz words in the sector, as well as phrases like 'fast-paced projects', 'high-energy environment', 'new ventures'
Market culture	
Results-orientated and competitive, e.g. FTSE 100 companies who have to report back to shareholders	Financial performance is the priority, so show how, directly or indirectly, you've made a contribution to this in the past
	Examples of using data to help you or the organisation make decisions, e.g. monthly performance reports
	Talk about 'targets', 'deadlines', 'revenue', 'competitor analysis', 'goals achieved', 'new business opportunities', etc.
Customer focus	
Prioritising needs of customers or clients, e.g. hospitality, healthcare	Examples of how you increased internal or external customer satisfaction levels and solved their problems
	Share experiences of working with similar customers to the ones in the companies you want to work for
	Talk about 'positive feedback and evaluation', 'repeat business', 'referrals through recommendations'

Organisational culture	Emphasise in your CV
Expert culture	
Organisations where knowledge is prized, e.g. universities, consultancies	Lead with your professional credentials, qualifications, expertise, specialisms and any publications or research
	Share how you've advised other people, internally or externally, and your continuous learning
	Use word and phrases like 'best-practice', 'world-class', 'industry-leading', 'accredited' to talk about your previous experiences
Creative	
Ideas, originality, aesthetics are important, e.g. design agencies and media	Present a visually interesting CV design with stylish format, fonts and even graphics (see Chapter 13)
	Show more personality, such as interesting hobbies, humour or quirky facts about you
	Name-drop prestigious brands, well-known people or high-profile projects to impress

Researching the employer's market

You only need to read the business news to see how organisations are continually adjusting to external pressures, such as changes in customer expectations, new legislation or technology opportunities.

An organisation's staff requirements will depend, for instance, on whether it's looking to grow the business, trying to keep its head above water or focusing on innovation to stay ahead.

You can find lots of information on the internet about trends and challenges in particular sectors, including reports from government and industry bodies, media news, as well as LinkedIn articles and discussions. It's also worth looking at similar companies in the field to see how they are faring.

Looking more widely at an employer's marketplace can help differentiate you as a candidate who understands and is interested in their bigger challenges, and that will set you apart from most other candidates who look no further than the job details provided.

Research channels
- Company websites
- Online salary surveys
- Sector reports
- Social media, including LinkedIn and Glassdoor
- News items and PR
- Professional associations
- Trade journals
- Agencies and headhunters
- Personal contacts

Researching for an online CV

The above research is going to be very helpful if you are applying to a specific organisation. However, if you are creating a CV that will be posted online for potentially lots of different employers and recruiters to see, then you need to do your research slightly differently.

Find five to six advertisements for the types of job you are interested in, and find the competencies and requirements they have in common and any other information that helps give you an insight into the type of candidate they all want. Make a note of the following in respect of their requirements:

- skills, knowledge and experience
- salary range
- qualifications/training
- key duties and responsibilities
- personal characteristics
- any other particular requirements.

For finding salary information, you can simply type in 'salary survey' and your job title or sector into a search engine, and you'll find lots of information on market rates from recruitment agencies.

Your professional association or trade journal is also likely to have information about recruitment trends for its members.

NB: job websites can give a false impression of the supply of actual jobs, because some recruitment agencies advertise in more than one place or don't remove filled jobs from their listings.

In addition, talk to people who know the field in which you want to work, whether it's a personal connection, someone you know indirectly or even a complete stranger on LinkedIn. Politely ask for their opinion and advice on what they would look for in candidates, and for any feedback about how you can improve your chances.

If you can talk to a recruitment agency or headhunter, they should also be able to tell you the skills and experience most in demand currently.

ACTIVITY 7: YOUR MARKET RESEARCH

Use this activity to gather your research together, ↓ then head online to **indigo.careers/standout_CVs** where you can input your answers for each company or role you are applying to into a downloadable form.

For specific job applications

Your research should include the following if you are applying for a particular role or organisation.

- Their origin story, evolution, values and ambitions for the future
- Size, locations, range of products, services or purpose
- Senior team and the hiring managers' profiles and background (check LinkedIn)
- Key customers and target audience
- Any standards it works to, e.g. quality, regulatory, or best practice
- Current challenges for the company and the sector as a whole
- How they compare with their competitors
- The organisation's culture or personality.

For an online CV

Find five to six advertisements for the roles you are interested in; from the job details and person specifications, note the candidate requirements they have in common and any differences, in particular:

- skills, knowledge and experience
- qualifications and training
- personal characteristics
- key duties and responsibilities
- salary and reward package.

This will give you a market insight into what employers are currently looking for when they recruit to those types of role. You can then build your online CV in a way that will appeal directly to them.

Use your research to:

- develop a CV or application that makes it easy for recruiters to see your suitability
- check whether you are being realistic in what you are looking for
- benchmark salary levels so that you know your earning potential
- ascertain if there is anything else that could give you a competitive edge. If so, go out and do it
- focus your energy on applying for roles that are most likely to be responsive to what you have to offer
- impress at interview with the enthusiasm and thoughtfulness of your research.

IN A NUTSHELL

This chapter has focused on the different ways you can research what an employer is looking for in a candidate. It has helped you to:

- check rather than assume that you know who the employer's ideal candidate is
- understand the other factors that might influence candidate selection
- use this research in your CV to help you stand out from other candidates.

PART THREE
DEVISING YOUR CV

CHAPTER 6
Choice language

CHAPTER 7
The first half page of your CV

CHAPTER 8
Chronological CVs

CHAPTER 9
Functional CVs

CHAPTER 10
One-page CVs

CHAPTER 11
Developing your own CV website

CHAPTER 12
Making your CV look good

CHAPTER 13
CVs for specific career challenges

What should your CV look and sound like?

Parts One and Two of this book helped you gather the content for your CV and understand specifically what your target employers are looking for.

Part Three is going to focus on the form, structure and tone of your CV. It will show you how different headings and formats for your CV can be used to make it easier for you to organise the information and for the employer to appreciate your suitability for the post.

Although you will find many different views on what a CV should look like, the truth is that as long as you follow three simple rules, there is flexibility in how you choose to display your CV.

Three rules for a winning CV:

1. Your CV should be well presented, clean and professional

2. Essential information, such as your contact details, career history and relevant qualifications, must be included

3. It should be easy for the employer to see why you are a suitable candidate.

Let's look at how we can help you achieve this.

6 CHOICE LANGUAGE

Finding the right words to use on your CV is not always easy. So, before we go on to write your CV, let's look at some tips and techniques to make this easier.

This chapter will help you:

- know how to refer to yourself within your CV
- find the right pitch – be confident but not over the top
- understand the key words that will get you noticed by recruiters.

Speaking volumes

The language you use in your CV works on many different levels; it:

- conveys factual content
- directly and indirectly expresses what the individual thinks about that content
- creates associations for the reader, some of which may be obvious, others more subtle.

Most importantly, careful and deliberate use of language in your CV can influence all of the above points in your favour.

This chapter looks at how you can use language cleverly within your CV to not only convey the factual information, but to reinforce an image in the employer's mind of you as an ideal candidate.

Me, myself and I

How you refer to yourself within the CV is going to influence what the reader thinks about you and how they think you view yourself — so choose wisely.

The 'I' option
This is used for a more formal approach, when you are writing in full sentences. However, it usually means that you have to repeatedly use the personal pronoun, as in, 'I did this' and 'I was responsible for that', which tends to look clumsy, egocentric and quickly becomes tiresome to read.

The 'we' option
Within an organisation, people frequently use the word 'we' in conversations, as there is often an emphasis on organisational teamwork. However, in recruitment, the employer is interested in what *you* did. If you use the pronoun 'we' within your CV or the interview, then it becomes unclear what contribution you made.

The third person option

Some CVs refer to the individual in the third person, as though someone else has written the CV on their behalf, e.g. 'Jones spent 10 years working with...'

If you are thinking of writing it in this style, then be careful. It frequently trips people up – they get themselves in all kinds of grammatical confusions and often start using the 'I' pronoun later on. There can also be a tendency to pile on the superlatives, e.g. 'Jones is a master of his craft...' However, most of the time we know Jones has written it, so this makes him look like a complete egomaniac.

It is appropriate to use this option if someone else really is writing it for you, e.g. a headhunter creating a profile for you, or something produced by your organisation as part of their sales and marketing, e.g. management consultancy.

Perhaps the easiest solution is to use bullet points led by strong action words, as illustrated in the comparison between a bullet point and full sentences below.

BULLET POINTS VERSUS FULL SENTENCES

• Repaired a difficult relationship with a stakeholder who had been unhappy with the previous post-holder; by ensuring quality delivery and scheduling regular updates, I was able to rebuild trust.	I encountered a challenging situation where a key stakeholder expressed deep dissatisfaction with the performance of the previous role incumbent. Recognising the critical importance of fostering positive relationships with stakeholders, I embarked on a mission to repair this strained connection and rebuild trust, with a proactive approach to ensuring the delivery of high quality services and products. I meticulously reviewed the existing processes and identified areas for improvement, encouraging feedback and actively seeking ways to enhance our deliverables.

Which do you think works best?

The bullet point is clean and succinct, with no personal pronoun. The formal paragraph is longer, clumsier, repeatedly uses 'I' and full sentences, which makes it seem long-winded. As Elvis one sang, '*A little less conversation and a little more action*' will stand you in good stead.

The magic of words

A study by the psychology department of the University of Hertfordshire showed that specific words and phrases used in CVs and application forms were a key influence in determining which candidates were shortlisted.

Positive, upbeat words sprinkled throughout your CV help reinforce the message that you are a high-performing, easy to work with, 'can-do' type of candidate – the kind that every employer wants.

Useful action words for your CV

accelerated	boosted	created
accomplished	briefed	cultivated
achieved	broadened	customised
adapted	built	decreased
advised	calculated	defeated
advocated	canvassed	defined
aligned	centralised	delivered
allocated	chaired	demonstrated
analysed	clarified	designed
applied	coached	determined
arbitrated	collaborated	developed
arranged	communicated	devised
assessed	compiled	diagnosed
attained	completed	differentiated
attracted	constructed	directed
audited	contributed	discovered
authored	controlled	disseminated
awarded	convinced	distinguished
balanced	coordinated	diversified

documented
doubled
drafted
educated
eliminated
enabled
encouraged
enforced
engineered
enhanced
enjoyed
enlarged
enriched
ensured
equipped
established
evaluated
examined
exhibited
expanded
experimented
explained
explored
extended
facilitated
filtered
finalised
fine-tuned
fixed
focused
forecast
formulated
fortified
founded
generated
guided
handled
harmonised

headed
helped
highlighted
identified
illustrated
implemented
improved
incorporated
increased
influenced
initiated
innovated
inspired
instigated
integrated
introduced
invested
investigated
launched
led
liaised
located
managed
marketed
maximised
mediated
mentored
minimised
mobilised
modernised
modified
monitored
motivated
navigated
negotiated
nurtured
operated
orchestrated

organised
originated
outlined
overcame
overhauled
oversaw
persuaded
piloted
pinpointed
pioneered
planned
prepared
presented
prioritised
promoted
proved
publicised
published
qualified
raised
ran
recommended
reconciled
recruited
rectified
reduced
refined
regulated
rehabilitated
reinforced
renewed
reorganised
repaired
replaced
researched
reshaped
resolved
restored

retained	sorted	transformed
revamped	spear-headed	translated
reviewed	specialised	uncovered
revitalised	standardised	unified
saved	straightened	unlocked
scheduled	streamlined	updated
secured	strengthened	upgraded
selected	structured	utilised
set goals	summarised	validated
set up	supervised	verified
shaped	supported	visualised
shared	surpassed	volunteered
simplified	taught	widened
sold	tested	won
solved	trained	wrote

Useful adverbs

accurately	cooperatively	proactively
assertively	creatively	promptly
astutely	decisively	quickly
capably	effectively	rapidly
carefully	efficiently	resourcefully
clearly	energetically	responsibly
cleverly	enthusiastically	selectively
collaboratively	ethically	sensitively
competently	inclusively	successfully
consistently	positively	vigilantly
consultatively	powerfully	

Use these and similar words to describe how you approached your tasks and achievements. The more positive words you can include, the more of a 'can-do' impression you will create.

Toxic words

Here are some other words that it is probably best to avoid in your CV, unless you are showing how you achieved a positive from a negative, e.g. 'successfully launched design previously thought **unworkable**'.

abandoned	fired	objectionable
absurd	fought	opposed
argued	futile	preposterous
attempted	gave up	recession
avoided	grievance	ridiculous
bullying	harassed	shoddy
bureaucratic	hopeless	slump
closed down	idiotic	stress
confined	impossible	stupid
conflicted	impractical	succumbed
criticised	incapable	tried
decline	inconceivable	ugly
decrease	indecisive	unbearable
defeated	ineffectual	unendurable
denied	inept	unmanageable
difficult	infuriating	unreasonable
disagreement	intolerable	unruly
disciplined	irreparable	unsuccessfully
dismissed	irreversible	unworkable
disorganised	isolated	weak
down-sized	lost	weird
empty	maddening	withdrew
exasperating	miserable	worrying
failed	non-viable	wrestled

Pitch perfect

The language used in your CV needs to be positive and confident — but not 'over the top'. How can you judge the difference? Compare the following sentences.

- Superb sales track record as the top performer in the team for the last two years, with an 80% conversion rate.
- Brilliant sales-person who always gets the sale, exceeding all targets set with unprecedented levels of success and profitability.

The first statement is anchored with data that substantiates the claim of a superb sales track record, with a comparison for reference. The second sentence may be equally true, but it seems like empty bragging without evidence to back it up.

If you are great at your job, then you do need to shout about it but prove it with examples, e.g.:

- Awarded 'Employee of the Month' for my exceptional customer service, including helping a customer who was so grateful they wrote to the company to express their thanks
- Exceptional co-ordination skills, scheduling over 100 site visits a week, ensuring staff are fully briefed, and the right equipment is available to reduce the need for return visits
- Trusted adviser, with 75% of my business generated from referrals from previous satisfied clients.

Technical words

Most industries or professional/technical jobs have their own jargon or buzz words. These should be used to show your relevant knowledge. However, often the person shortlisting is not a technical expert, so care needs to be taken that they can understand what you are talking about.

It is safe and desirable to use jargon that has already been used in the job description or advertisement. Where you describe in detail other technical skills or knowledge, make sure that you clearly link it to a particular skill or competence described in the job description or advertisement so a non-technical recruiter can see its relevance.

Keyword search

When using recruitment sites you have two audiences to convince, the recruitment software and the human who is ultimately going to invite you to interview and hopefully offer you the job.

However, if the software doesn't pick you up as a potential candidate then you are never going to get the chance to impress in person.

Recruiters generate a list of potential candidates by using keywords to search through the candidate databases for suitable people. This makes the words you include on your CV of great importance.

How can you anticipate what keywords the recruiter may be looking for?

For specific roles, if you look carefully at the job advert and job descriptions they will normally tell you exactly what is needed. Also your research on the company, culture and the sector it operates in will reveal more clues about how to position yourself as someone who will fit in. Look back at Chapter 2 and the activities you completed as a reminder.

You can also ask AI. When applying for a specific role you can copy in the job advert and job description and ask it '*What do you think are the keywords that a recruiter will use to search for suitable candidates for this role?*' It will then give you a summarised list of what it sees as the standout priorities.

When writing a CV for use on recruitment sites rather than a specific job, you should widen the search and ask it '*What selection criteria and keywords are most likely to be used by a recruiter to find candidates for a (insert role)?*' It will then tell you the commonly used keywords for those types of roles.

Here's an example. I asked AI: *'What keywords are used to rank candidates for a customer service role?'*

AI response: *'When ranking candidates for a customer service role, here are some common keywords that recruiters might use:'*

active listening	*conflict resolution*	*multi-tasking*
adaptability	*customer care*	*patience*
call center (NB the American spelling)	*customer interaction*	*problem-solving*
	customer service	*service-oriented*
client service	*customer support*	*teamwork*
communication skills	*empathy*	*technical support*
complaint handling	*help desk*	*time management*

These are useful keywords to thread into your CV. You can also copy your CV, along with the anticipated keywords, into the AI prompt and ask it to re-edit your CV with examples and achievements that use those keywords.

As always, you will need to edit and personalise the responses from the AI to make it relevant and factually accurate. You will also notice from the list the American spellings of words such as 'call center', so you will need to adjust these.

Whatever approach you take, it's important to take the time to weave relevant keywords throughout your CV with lots of practical examples to show these aren't just empty words but reflect your genuine experience. It's not enough to include them just as random words in a list.

ACTIVITY 8: KEYWORD SELECTION

1 Review the person specification details and job description for roles that interest you, and note the keywords likely to be used by recruiters to sift applicants.

2 Ask AI to help you generate likely keywords and desirable competencies for these types of roles.

3 Identify the technical words or jargon that you can use to show your expertise, but ensure that they are placed in a context that a non-technical recruiter could understand – or at least in a way that directly mirrors the wording in a person specification.

4 ⬇ Use the activity form available online at **indigo.careers/standout_CVs** to save this information for later use.

IN A NUTSHELL

This chapter has focused on helping you choose language that will support and complement the content of your CV. Remember to:

- use positive language throughout your CV, including action-orientated and positive descriptive words and phrases, e.g. 'created' or 'managed sensitively'
- use negative words only if showing how you improved the situation, e.g. 'achieved 30% sales increase for a product line that had previously performed badly'
- always provide evidence of any claims about your excellent performance
- find and use the keywords that are going to get you noticed by recruiters
- results-orientated bullet points reinforce the sense of energy in the CV and help avoid the over-use of the 'I' or 'we' pronoun
- technical CVs should be understandable by a non-technical person who has only the person specification in front of them
- pare down the detail to the bare minimum: avoid flowery and over-wordy sentences.

7 THE FIRST HALF PAGE OF YOUR CV

This is the most important part of your CV because it will determine whether the rest of it is read by the employer or not. You need to create an opening for your CV that is both functional and immediately gains the employer's interest.

This chapter will help you:

- ensure your personal information is in a format that is compatible with recruitment software

- succinctly convey your professional profile or personal brand

- write a career profile that will grab the employer's attention.

Your CV is essentially a sales document. The aim is to generate the employer's interest so that they will invite you to an interview. You are competing not only with other applicants, but also with the short attention spans of recruiters. Typically, an employer will glance at your CV and within seconds make a judgement about whether to read any further. Where recruitment software is used, then you've literally nanoseconds to convince the software that you're a candidate who should be ranked highly enough for a human recruiter to even bother reading.

The first half page has to grab their attention, so if you bury all of your rich career experience on page 2, you are likely to end up on the reject pile.

> *When I'm recruiting for a specific role, I'm not interested in reading a CV that is an autobiography or where I have to work out how the candidate is suitable. While I appreciate a lot of time and effort goes into putting together a CV, I expect the candidate to have done that work for me otherwise, unfortunately, they are usually on the reject pile. Remember, your CV has to market you for a specific job and therefore needs to be focused, rather than trying to be all things to all people.*
>
> Clare Burles, HR Director

Your CV headings

There is one heading that you are not going to need. Do not head your CV with either 'Curriculum Vitae' or 'Résumé'. It's not wrong, just old-fashioned. There is also a danger that if this is the first heading on your CV, a computer could scan your name as 'Ms Curriculum Vitae'.

Personal information

Your name
This should always be at the very top of your CV, usually in a bigger font than the rest of the CV, e.g. size 14 if you are using 12 elsewhere. You could also use capital letters.

Address
Recruiters want to know where you live, even if the role is fully remote.

It's no longer recommended to put your full address on your CV, given there are cases of criminals using recruitment sites for identity theft. Instead, just put the city or town you're based in or the first part of your post code. This will ensure that your location information is stored on the candidate database, so that if the recruiter is looking for more local candidates, your CV will be included. If you don't include any location information you may not appear in the recruiter's search results, even if the job is around the corner.

Telephone number
Share your mobile number, and make sure there is a professional sounding voicemail ready to record messages.

Email address
Use your personal email address or, ideally, set up an email address solely for your job-searching activities. This should include your name and perhaps your field of work. These rules ensure that you don't get confused with anyone else and they don't mistype your email.

Rights to work in the country
If there might be any query regarding your rights to work in the country to which you are applying, then it's useful to state up-front that you either have full rights or the conditions on which they are based.

Format
CVs that are uploaded to a recruitment website are 'parsed' by recruitment software. This means your CV document is broken down into data components and then extracted to a database that stores the information in separate fields. The database can then be used to search fields for content that matches the recruiter's requirements.

This makes it very important that your CV can be easily parsed. Recruitment software will normally assume that your name and contact details are at the very top of your CV. However, even if you have put these details in the appropriate place, if you have heavily formatted them – perhaps using an unusual font or graphic – then these details may not be parsed correctly; it is far better to use a very plain format for your contact details.

Examples of layout for personal information

Hanif Kotecha
Sawbridge, SW9
Email: hkotecha@gmail.com
Mobile: 07771 777 555

John Brown

Email:	johnb@yahoo.com
Mobile:	+44 07772 666 555
Location:	Gladstown, South Africa
Work status:	Full rights to work in the UK due to dual citizenship

Writing a career profile

A career profile is a mini-advertisement that is placed directly after your personal details to try to capture the attention of the employer by summarising why you are a great candidate. It consists of approximately three to five sentences describing the skills, knowledge and experience you have that are relevant to the job sought. It usually sits in its own section on the first page, situated directly under the personal contact details.

Recruitment software will rank CVs more highly when it finds the keywords it is looking for early on in the CV and if they are backed up with the same or similar keyword mentions later on. This is because it assumes that if you describe yourself using those words at the start and then reinforce these later, it's an accurate reflection of who you are professionally.

This is why it's so important to create a profile using the keywords likely to be used as search terms by recruiters, rather than producing a general introduction or no introduction at all.

Let's look at the different elements needed in your career profile. You will find the activities you completed in Parts One and Two to be very helpful.

Job title

Employees can get very hot under the collar about job titles and what they feel their role should be called. However, job titles are notoriously misleading. There is no standardisation across organisations about job titles. Even departments within the same organisation sometimes use job titles differently. Recruiters will look to benchmark your experience by looking at your scope of responsibilities and your pay level, rather than from your job title alone.

However, given this, wherever possible, use the title of the job you are applying for to describe yourself within the career profile. If they are looking for a 'customer services assistant', then call yourself this even if your previous job title was actually 'customer liaison officer'. This is justifiable if your previous roles have been similar in function, even if your job title is listed slightly differently in your career history. This will make it far easier for recruitment software to find you and for recruiters to immediately see your suitability. Of course this has to be substantiated by the rest of your CV; it's no use calling yourself 'customer services manager' when your CV shows no evidence of management skills.

Key experience

The career profile should include how many years' experience you have in the area they are looking for. For example:

- sales adviser with 2 years' sales experience within the computer retail sector
- teacher with 5 years' post-qualification experience working internationally
- technical engineer with over 25 years' experience working within the UK telecommunications sector.

Relevant qualifications, education, professional affiliations

Include relevant professional qualifications and memberships in your profile. For example:

- Nursery Assistant with NVQ level 3 in Childcare
- Member of the Chartered Institute of Marketing (MCIM)
- RCIS qualified surveyor
- MBA qualified business analyst.

Key knowledge

Describe any relevant specialist knowledge you have. For example:

- organising trade exhibitions
- industry expert on network architecture
- specialist in crime prevention for businesses
- excellent knowledge of arboriculture.

Relevant training

Include any training that supports your work. For example:

- trained mediator
- trained in health and safety risk assessments
- trained in CAD design.

Personal attributes

As we have seen in Part One, employers do like to get a sense of what you are like as a person/employee.

Many candidates will include in their career profile some personality traits that they think will impress the employer, such as 'dynamic', 'team player' or 'strong communication skills'.

However, without evidence to back these up, they are pretty meaningless and unlikely to give you a competitive edge when 95% of other candidates claim to have these attributes too. You need to be much more specific on how these characteristics express themselves at work (see Table 9, opposite, for ideas).

TABLE 9: INSTEAD OF 'STRONG COMMUNICATION SKILLS' SPECIFY THE TYPE OF COMMUNICATION SKILLS YOU HAVE

Verbal skills	Written skills
Persuading individuals	Advising others
Influencing stakeholders	Accuracy in recording data
Selling to customers	Story-telling
Presenting to an audience	Minute-taking
Mediating conflict	Research and referencing
Negotiating in person	Writing copy for promotional materials
Handling conflicts	Producing instruction manuals
Making visitors feel welcome	Creating articles on topical issues
Relationship building	Diplomatic and sensitive correspondence
Translating	Legal and commercial agreements
Advocacy	Writing policies and procedures
Training and coaching	Editing and proofreading

Review your research from Parts One and Two of this book. What kind of person is the employer looking for? Focus on identifying the particular interpersonal skills and abilities that you think they want, and use your own experience to demonstrate you have them (see Table 10 below).

TABLE 10: PROVE YOUR INTERPERSONAL SKILLS AND ABILITIES

Good negotiator ✘	Highly experienced in negotiating favourable contract terms with software suppliers ✓
Strong communication skills ✘	Articulate and persuasive communicator, winning funding and resources for our campaign ✓
Excellent written skills ✘	Adept at making complex subjects accessible to a wider audience, including scientific information for school children ✓
Relationship building ✘	Strong relationship-building skills that have resulted in three of our biggest customers increasing their orders by 25% ✓

Additional information

The career profile is also a good place to briefly mention any other impressive information that positions you as a high-performing, must-see candidate. For example:

- outstanding student achievements
- awards won or nominated for
- prestigious companies, customers, VIP individuals or high-profile projects you have been involved with
- media appearances, industry recognition, research or publications
- languages spoken
- being a volunteer mentor or brand ambassador.

If there is something that is particularly impressive or even interestingly quirky that shows you in a good light, include this in the career profile.

Let's now thread the following elements together for your career profile.

- Job title
- Years of experience
- Relevant career history and skills
- Impressive achievements, projects or people.

EXAMPLES OF CAREER PROFILES

- Talented Graphic Design graduate, skilled in using Adobe Creative Suite to craft visually compelling designs for company branding and digital platforms. Deep understanding of user-centred design principles (UX Design), brand identity and visual story-telling. My combination of visual imagination and good listening skills enables me to transform clients' requirements into authentic and innovative designs that exceed expectations. This has resulted in superb feedback from the projects I worked on in my placement year and in a Distinction for my end of year University assignment.

- Highly organised and detail-oriented Administrator with 5 years' experience working in healthcare settings including the NHS. Excellent co-ordination skills developed from scheduling clinics requiring complex logistics. Diligent in ensuring compliance with rigorous governance

> processes including accurately processing sensitive data. Adept at working in high-pressure environments where team-working is key and in providing empathetic support to anxious patients at challenging times. Excellent IT and database management skills.
>
> - Agile Technical Manager with over 10 years' experience working with fast-paced organisations in the telecommunications sector including the market leader X-mobile. Extensive knowledge of cutting-edge technologies and a successful track record in overseeing the rollout of innovative products from inception to in-store delivery. Instrumental in driving the successful launch of the record-breaking Zeto range, the market's fastest-selling product of the year. Also led on the development of a range of accessories that boosted turnover by £50 million to date. Proven leadership at the forefront of innovation.

Writing a career objective statement

A career objective statement can be can be added to your career profile statement. Simply put, it says what kind of job you are looking for and why.

A career objective statement is particularly helpful when:

- you have just left school or university and have little or no work experience
- you are applying to a company with lots of potential routes
- you don't want to be pigeon-holed in the area that your CV suggests
- you are applying for promotion and want to justify why you are suitable even if you do not have all of the experience required for working at the new level
- you are posting your CV on a public website and want to be clear about the kinds of roles you are interested in
- you are sending your CV speculatively to organisations.

Some examples of career objective statements are given below.

- Experienced programme developer seeking a role where I can combine my technical expertise and creative skills within a research and development-focused team.
- Education professional looking for opportunities to help people learn within a corporate environment.

- Following completion of my Certificate in CIPD, I am looking for a role in an HR department where my people skills would be an asset.

The disadvantage of career objective statements is that if you state too narrow a job focus, it could mean that you exclude yourself from other potentially interesting opportunities which the employer could have in mind. Also, if you choose to include a career objective statement, then make sure that the job you say you are looking for is compatible with the one for which you have just applied.

> **USING AI TO HELP YOU WRITE YOUR CAREER PROFILE**
>
> - Using the Chat function, ask: 'Give me five examples of career profiles for a CV for a...' (insert job title).
>
> - List the elements that you want to include in your profile, e.g. your job title, specific qualifications, skills and experience, and achievements. Ask the AI to use the information to write three versions of this profile for your CV. If they are too long, you can ask it to do a more concise version.
>
> - AI is very helpful for providing a structure and ideas that you can build on and personalise to make completely your own.

ACTIVITY 9: WRITING A CAREER PROFILE

It's now your turn to start writing your CV career profile. ⬇ You can download this activity from **indigo.careers/standout_CVs** and experiment with different versions.

1. Look through your research from Part One to help you cherry-pick your relevant career experience, significant achievements and personal qualities.

2. Review your research from Part Two to focus on your target employer's key requirements. Aim to show in your statement how you meet these.

3. Write four to five carefully crafted sentences with a confident tone.

> **4** Describe yourself with a job title that is in keeping with the roles you are applying for and which you can justify.
>
> **5** Remember to keep all claims factual and specific with evidence.
>
> **6** Experiment with AI to create different versions.

Now let's start writing the main body of your CV. The following chapters present a number of different CV formats you can use. Read through the chapters to decide which of these suits you best.

IN A NUTSHELL

This chapter has helped you write the first half page of your CV so that you:

- can follow a recruitment software-friendly format to write your CV headings, including contact details
- know what personal information to include
- can write your career profile in a way that ensures your CV is easily found by recruiters and which will impress them quickly with your suitability.

8 CHRONOLOGICAL CVs

A chronological CV format is one where your work history, qualifications, etc. are displayed in reverse chronological order. This means that your most recent employment appears first on the CV and it works its way backwards to your first job.

It is a straightforward CV format to write, as it is organised in a very logical way. However, depending on your work history and target role, there are other formats that may help you to sell your skills more effectively. This and each of the following chapters will cover a different CV format. You can choose to present your CV in one or more of these formats, depending on which suits you best.

This chapter will help you:

- understand when to use a chronological CV
- write your CV in this format.

A chronological CV organises its content according to a historical timeline. Employers like them because they can see very easily what your work history and career progression has been. They can also see any career breaks, the length of each employment and any changes in career path.

If you are looking for a role that is a natural progression given your career to date, then the chronological CV format will be appropriate, and will highlight your suitability for the role; for example, a conference assistant who is looking for a similar role in the same industry or for the next step up.

Under your most recent employment, it should be possible to demonstrate relevant skills and experience that the employer will be interested in. It is also helpful in highlighting the names of your previous employers. This can be advantageous if they are prestigious brands or competitors of your target employer, and therefore likely in themselves to attract interest.

However, if your last employment(s) have not been directly relevant to the role you are applying for, then a chronological CV will do you no favours. It will instead raise questions about why you are applying. Equally, if you have had several jobs, gaps between jobs or career breaks, then this CV format could make what is a very legitimate work history look potentially troublesome. In this case, you would be advised to look at one of the other CV formats, such as a functional CV, which is covered in the next chapter.

Let's look at how you would write a chronological CV using all of the information you have gathered when doing the activities in this book.

PROS AND CONS OF CHRONOLOGICAL CVs

Advantages of a chronological CV

- A chronological format is liked by most employers.
- It is a clear and simple format.
- It is easy to chart your career progression, e.g. promotions or growing specialisation.

Disadvantages of a chronological CV

- A chronological CV will show up any inconsistencies or variations in your career path.
- It can reveal unimportant or inconsequential jobs.
- It can reveal periods of unemployment or brief job tenure.

Advantages of a chronological CV	Disadvantages of a chronological CV
• It is more in line with application forms with experience, dates, employment history laid out in a straightforward manner.	• It may emphasise your lack of wider experience if you have stayed in one job for a long time.

Template for a chronological CV

Name

Location:
Tel.:
Email:

Career profile
(Use or adapt the career profile you wrote in Activity 9)
Describe yourself using the same or a similar title to the job you are applying for and give details of your experience in the sector. Follow with a few lines (approximately three to five) which summarise what you have to offer in relation to the job, e.g. key skills and experience. Include a mix of technical, professional and softer skills. Include prestigious brand names, awards, etc. Your profile is the most important part of your CV and it should encourage a prospective employer to read further.

Career history
(Use material from Activity 1 on information gathering and from Activity 7 for your research on matching you to the role)

Most recent job titleOrganisationDate (year to year)
- Write a brief description: one to two sentences on the company, its size, products, location, structure (Activity 1).
- Describe your key achievements in your last post, bearing in mind the requirements for the job you are applying for. Quantify those achievements – what difference did it make to the organisation? (Activity 5)
- Do not write your job description here – cherry-pick skills and duties and personal qualities relevant to the role being sought.

Previous job titleOrganisationDate
Previous job titleOrganisationDate
Previous job titleOrganisationDate
Previous job titleOrganisationDate

Go back 10–15 years or more if your jobs prior to this still have relevance to the job for which you are applying. You can give fewer details the further back you go. Try not to repeat yourself. If you are in danger of doing this, a functional CV may be more appropriate.

If you need to write about a period where you had several jobs but do not wish to go into specifics you could group them together as 'a variety of roles, including Project Manager, Team Leader, Team Coordinator, which enabled the development of my ...'

Qualifications and training
- List relevant professional qualifications/memberships first, e.g. Trained NVQ Assessor.
- Higher academic qualifications should be listed before others unless lower qualifications are of more immediate relevance.
- School qualifications do not need to be included on the CV where you have higher qualifications.
- Training can be a separate heading. Do not list all training courses but do include those that may have a direct benefit on new employers, e.g. first aid, project management.

Additional information
- This section can be used to include any information that will show you in a good light as a candidate.
- You might like to include any voluntary work that you do, e.g. school governor.
- You can also include language skills, clean driving licence, inventions, achievements outside work.

Interests
This is optional, but can be useful if you have limited work experience and want to give the employer more of a sense about what you are like as a person. Also if you are more 'mature' in years, you can use this section to show that you are fit, energetic and up to date.

The CV should be no more than two pages long unless you need to include lists of publications, research or multiple projects.

CV 1: Chronological CV

Chris Perkins

Address: Fensworth LB1
Tel: 01234 555666
Mobile: 07774 777666
E-mail: cperkins@gmail.co.uk

Career profile
Commercial manager and CIMA qualified accountant, with over 20 years' experience of working within health sector organisations undergoing merger and acquisition. Track record of adding significant value to organisations as a result of rigorous analysis, creative problem-solving and identifying lucrative business opportunities which would otherwise have been missed. This includes the acquisition of a major new hospital as part of Cortins' ambitious growth strategy and advising on investments for Koppen and RST group. Highly knowledgeable about the sector, its financial operations and challenges, and how to develop robust, win-win commercial solutions for patients and shareholders.

Employment history
Regional Commercial Manager   Cortins Healthcare Ltd   2021 to date

Responsible for financial performance of three hospitals with combined turnover of £265 million for Cortins Healthcare Ltd, one of the largest private healthcare providers in the UK.

- Met service delivery targets and budget for all the hospitals under my remit.
- Identified Lady Godwin Hospital as a key target acquisition and as a key member of the bid team, succeeded in acquiring it for £2 million less than requested purchase price.
- Negotiated and agreed fees with hospital consultants. This was a sensitive issue that was crucial to the continued effectiveness and profitability of the organisation.
- Devised strategic plan for continued growth based on in-depth benchmarking exercise, which was adopted by the Board.
- Improved the user-friendliness of the financial information available to department heads and supported managers in developing action plans.
- Negotiated new service-level agreement with cleaning company which addressed service shortfalls and provided ongoing monitoring to ensure service standards.

Business Analyst   Koppen Insurance   2017–2021
Koppen Insurance is an international insurance company with a turnover of £300 million, providing diverse insurance products. My role was to grow the financial performance of the new health insurance segment of the business.
- Wrote strategic plan for expansion into private healthcare market, which was approved by the Board and subsequently brought in over £10 million profit into the company within the first year.
- Handled the selling of the unprofitable investment business, preparing all due diligence paperwork, TUPE (Transfer of Undertakings (Protection of Employment) Regulations) transfer, etc.
- Trained new departmental heads in financial management and organisational financial processes.
- Led cross-organisational working group to review service delivery resulting in implementation of several recommendations including re-contracting with NHS providers.

Management Accountant   RST Group   2009–2017
Responsible for financial accounting processes for the rapidly expanding RST Group. They grew from £10 million revenues to £65 million in the four years I was with them.
- Integrated over 10 new corporate acquisitions into RST's financial processes.
- Trained and briefed staff in financial operating procedures.
- Worked closely with managers to set realistic budgets and delivery targets built on well-researched projections.
- Involved in financial accounting for all start-ups, acquisitions, extensions, new builds, conversions and product development strategies of the new business growth team.
- Prepared and presented business cases and investment appraisals to the investment committee which led to the development of two brand new services, one of which has since become responsible for over 20% of total revenue.
- Revised internal audit procedures and conducted regular internal audits.

Financial Consultant   Jones Consulting   2003–2009
Worked for Jones Consulting on several financial projects within the healthcare sector.
- Conducted financial review and assisted in strategy formulation for several NHS primary care trusts.
- Worked in compliance roles on several projects, including blue-chip companies such as DEF and GHI.

Qualifications
CIMA qualified   (first-time pass)
BSc Applied Physics (2:i) Smalltown University

IT skills
Advanced user of Excel, Pegasus, Agresso, Microsoft Office, SQL.

IN A NUTSHELL

Use a chronological CV when:

- last few roles/employers are directly relevant to job being sought
- you have been promoted and/or been given additional responsibilities throughout your career
- you can demonstrate steady employment and few employment gaps
- you can use well-known companies or prestigious brands to show your calibre.

Don't use a chronological CV when:

- seeking to downplay any career breaks or gaps between employment
- employment includes several short-term jobs, which could look like job-hopping
- you want to change career direction from previous career history
- your responsibilities have decreased in the course of your career, e.g. demotions.

9 FUNCTIONAL CVs

A functional CV format offers a highly flexible way of presenting your career history. Unlike a chronological CV, it is not structured by dates but by prioritising the information that is going to sell you most effectively to your target employer.

This chapter will help you:

- understand what a functional CV is and when to use it
- write your CV in this format.

A functional CV format will enable you to highlight in the first page of your CV the skills and experience you have that are of most relevance to the employer. This can include paid and unpaid work, transferable skills, qualifications or any other additional information which will demonstrate your suitability.

This is a particular advantage if you know you have the skills and experience to do the job, but your current or past employment has been in an unrelated role. Where an employer has detailed specific competencies that are required, you can also use these competencies as headings and provide examples with accompanying evidence.

You can select any of the following types of headings and order them according to how they will sell you best.

- career profile
- career history
- work experience
- key achievements
- key skills
- project experience
- IT skills
- education
- qualifications
- training
- innovations
- publications
- additional information
- hobbies/interests
- specialist knowledge
- positions of responsibility.

Depending on your experience and the job in question, it may make sense to prioritise some areas rather than others. For example, for jobs in the higher education or research sector, it makes sense to put your educational details first and then include headings for any publications, research, conference speeches and continuous professional development activities, etc. If you are selling yourself as an IT technical expert, you should specify your technical skills and knowledge up-front.

Chronological detail regarding your employment history is generally relegated to the second page. This means that any gaps in employment, unconnected jobs, etc. are downplayed as you will hopefully have persuaded the employer on the first page that you are suitable for shortlisting.

PROS AND CONS OF FUNCTIONAL CVs

Advantages of a functional CV

- It prioritises the areas of most relevance to the employer.
- You can combine skills and experience used in different jobs to strengthen what could otherwise come across as rather thin experience.
- You can use paid and unpaid work experience to support your application.
- You can omit or downplay any work history that could be seen as a distraction.
- Employment gaps or lots of short-term jobs are not as noticeable as in a chronological CV.
- It allows you to show your transferable skills, which is essential if you are seeking to change career direction or are a less than obvious candidate.

Disadvantages of a functional CV

- Employers are slightly more suspicious of this format given its usefulness in hiding things that the candidate would rather the employer didn't know.
- You will still need to supply the detail of employment dates, qualifications, etc. because the employer will want verification of whom you worked for and when.
- It can sometimes be unclear about the skills you gained from a particular job or experience.
- If you have had good career progression in an appropriate field, a functional CV will not show this as well as a chronological CV.
- It can be tricky to get the balance of information right and not make the CV too long.

If you feel that the functional format is a good format for your CV, then you can follow the template provided on the following pages and use the two sample CVs as a guide.

Template for a functional CV

Name

Location:
Tel.:
Email:

Career profile
(Use or adapt the career profile you wrote in Activity 9)
Describe yourself using the same or a similar title to the job you are applying for and give details of your experience in the sector. Follow with a few sentences (approximately three to five) that summarise what you have to offer to the job, e.g. key skills and experience. Your profile is the most important part of your CV and should encourage a prospective employer to read further.

Key skills and experience/key achievements or other relevant heading
Career history
(Use research from all the activities matching you to the role)
- From reading the advertisement or person specification for the job, show directly how you meet the selection criteria, choosing examples of how you demonstrate the competencies required.
- Put the information in bullet points, putting those most relevant to the job you are applying for at the top.
- Think of the skills you have developed from different jobs and even from activities outside work that show the competencies the employer is looking for.
- You can also include subheadings that match the selection criteria, e.g. financial management, training, etc.
- Include a mix of technical, professional and interpersonal skills.
- Include memberships or affiliations as appropriate.
- For key achievements, use the information you gained from Activities 4 and 5 in Chapter 3 to pick out two or three particular achievements that show your capabilities for the role, e.g. if the employer wants organisational skills, choose an example that shows these off to good effect.
- Quantify those achievements, e.g. increased sales by 30% over 2 months.
- This section will probably take up most of the first page.

Career summary

Most recent job title	Organisation	year to year
Previous job title	Organisation	year to year
Previous job title	Organisation	year to year

You can summarise your jobs or put a couple of lines about key responsibilities under each one.
If you need to include a period where you had several jobs but do not wish to go into specifics you could group them together, e.g. '2021–2022, worked in a variety of office-based roles, including PA and Customer Support, which helped me develop my administrative skills and my IT capabilities.'

Qualifications and training
- If a qualification is highly relevant include it in the career profile or on the first page. Otherwise list relevant professional qualifications/memberships first, e.g. Trained NVQ Assessor.
- Higher academic qualifications should be listed before others unless lower qualifications are of more immediate relevance.
- School qualifications do not need to be included on the CV where you have higher qualifications.
- Do not list all training courses but do include those that may have a direct benefit for new employers, e.g. first aid, project management.
- Remember training does not have to take place in a classroom to have value, e.g. distance learning, e-learning.

Other information
This may include any other relevant information, e.g. clean driving licence, languages, and any other piece of information which is significant.

Interests
This is optional. Three or four are usually sufficient but do think about whether you would be happy to talk about them and what they say about you. Make sure that they genuinely are your interests.

The CV should be no more than two pages long unless you need to include lists of publications or research.

CV 2: Functional CV (for a candidate with career gaps)

Nita Choudry

Northport, SS5
Mobile: 07777 777555
Email: nitac@gmail.com

Travel specialist with 10 years' experience ensuring clients arrive at their destination on time and with minimum stress. My experience includes arranging private flights for Board level and VIP guests, and organising corporate group travel and retail package holiday solutions. Extensive knowledge of GDS travel systems, including Sabre and Amadeus. Adept at dealing with demanding customers, finding workable solutions and crisis handling for travellers. Well-connected and knowledgeable about all aspects of travel, including how to find the best deals and call in favours when needed.

Key skills and experience
- Consistently the top performer within the travel team for my outstanding sales achievements and exceptional customer service, bringing in 50% of the business within a sales team of four.
- Built new partnerships with professional institutes such as DWA and NWR offering preferential rates to members, which brought in an estimated £50k additional revenue each year.
- Highly experienced in devising personalised itineraries to meet the exacting demands of VIP travellers, from transport to accommodation, entertainment and other concierge services.
- Achieving best value for corporate spend, negotiating an estimated £20k cost saving on a corporate customer's conference travel and accommodation costs.
- Expertise in creating secure travel programmes for visitors to high-risk areas, involving meticulous planning, vetting of local providers, full traveller briefing, training and instruction guides.
- Adept at crisis-handling, from clients losing passports or being arrested to hospitalisations during the pandemic in a foreign country.
- Received multiple online positive reviews from satisfied clients throughout my career, highlighting exceptional customer service, helpfulness and my ability to anticipate their needs.
- Able to advise clients on all aspects of travel, from visa requirements, health measures, legal, insurance and safety obligations, as well as consumer protection.
- BTEC National Diploma in Travel and Tourism.
- Excellent IT skills, including extensive knowledge of GDS systems and Microsoft Word.
- Language skills include English, French and Spanish, and currently learning Italian.

Employment history
Travel Representative   Conway Travel (ABTA registered)   2017–2020
Managed the corporate travel accounts for this local independent travel business.
- Helped manage the emergency repatriation of 200 clients during the pandemic: organising special transport and accommodation, quarantine arrangements requiring close liaison with government and health officials, their company and the individuals' families.
- Achieved a 10% increase in revenue by building new partnerships with professional membership bodies, upselling premium travel packages and from satisfied clients making repeat bookings.
- Managed over 50 corporate travel accounts, including investment banks, tech firms and charities, organising their travel plans, monitoring costs and taking into account traveller needs, including health information and personal preferences.
- Won £12k financial compensation for company travel claims due to cancelled flights, overcoming initial reluctance by the companies to offer full refunds.
- Worked with several corporates to devise staff performance incentives, including holiday prizes, wellbeing breaks and luxury experiences.
- Curated and arranged many personalised tours for professionals, both in the UK and further afield, e.g. ancient Turkey, wildlife experiences in South Africa and island hopping in Greece.

Travel Manager   Getaway Travel (ABTA registered)   2014–2015
An independent travel agency specialising in retail package holidays.
- Advised and arranged package, fly-drive and specialist holidays, as well as organising more bespoke packages.
- Liaised with tour operators to broker best value deals and devise unique upgrade offerings, extending customer choice.
- Organised specialist holidays for 'niche' audiences, including golf, cooking and yoga, which extended the travel season.
- Handled traveller emergencies, including hospitalisations, erupting volcanoes and lost passports, liaising with the local consulate, family members and quickly organising alternative arrangements with the hotel and travel companies.

Travel Assistant   Ultimate Holiday Company   2012–2014
These were the market leaders in leisure travel, and I was fortunate to receive excellent in-house training in all aspects of being a travel agent.
- Organising travel arrangements for leisure customers.
- Chasing up and checking tickets, schedules and documentation requirements.
- Creating bespoke packages in line with customer preferences.

Education and training
- BTEC National Diploma in Travel and Tourism.
- Training in customer service, sales and influencing.

Interests
- Travel, learning Italian, weight lifting.

CV 3: Functional CV (for a candidate who has taken a career detour into Health and Safety and wants to return to Training)

Gillian Knight

Lampshire, HM1
Mobile: 07983 999999
Email: gknight@googlemail.com

Learning and Development professional, qualified in CIPD and NEBOSH, focused on delivering employee development that significantly enhances employee performance, fosters career agility and reduces organisational risks. This includes creating management and soft skills training, as well as the health and safety courses that were so business-critical during the Covid-19 pandemic. As a trained coach with excellent communication skills, I excel in facilitating learner conversations and creating impactful learning content, as well as conducting training needs diagnostics to establish the real learning need and best mode of delivery. Adept at using learning management systems and evaluating outcomes to track return on investment.

Relevant experience history

Training design

- Successfully identified skills gaps and performance improvement opportunities through consultations with 30+ stakeholders, facilitation of three focus groups, and analysis of pulse surveys. Resulted in the implementation of a more blended learning approach, leading to a 10% increase in learner participation.
- Collaborated closely with external specialists to create tailored compliance training modules specific to our company, enabling much more successful transfer of learning into the workplace, as shown by end of year assessments.
- Designed an employee wellbeing campaign, which included training up 30 managers and six internal mental health first aiders, curating e-learning resources and providing signposting to our Employee Assistance Programme (which saw an 8% increase in referrals, helping people to get the support they need).
- Created comprehensive training materials, such as presentations, manuals, video instruction guides, and a WhatsApp learning group to continue conscientiousness about new learning and share experiences and queries.

Training delivery

- Trained coach and a mentor for Graduate and Apprenticeship programmes, guiding and supporting emerging talent in their career journey.
- Expertise in delivering both in-person workshops and virtual training sessions, utilising various interactive tools available in virtual platforms (e.g., whiteboards, surveys, chat functions).
- Successfully onboarded over 50 new employees each year through a combination of e-learning modules, virtual webinars and on-the-job demonstrations.
- Delivered a manual handling course to over 200 staff members, resulting in a significant reduction of up to 35% in injury reports among previously high-risk teams.

Employment history
Travel Representative　　Conway Travel (ABTA registered)　　2017–2020

Managed the corporate travel accounts for this local independent travel business.
- Helped manage the emergency repatriation of 200 clients during the pandemic: organising special transport and accommodation, quarantine arrangements requiring close liaison with government and health officials, their company and the individuals' families.
- Achieved a 10% increase in revenue by building new partnerships with professional membership bodies, upselling premium travel packages and from satisfied clients making repeat bookings.
- Managed over 50 corporate travel accounts, including investment banks, tech firms and charities, organising their travel plans, monitoring costs and taking into account traveller needs, including health information and personal preferences.
- Won £12k financial compensation for company travel claims due to cancelled flights, overcoming initial reluctance by the companies to offer full refunds.
- Worked with several corporates to devise staff performance incentives, including holiday prizes, wellbeing breaks and luxury experiences.
- Curated and arranged many personalised tours for professionals, both in the UK and further afield, e.g. ancient Turkey, wildlife experiences in South Africa and island hopping in Greece.

Travel Manager　　Getaway Travel (ABTA registered)　　2014–2015

An independent travel agency specialising in retail package holidays.
- Advised and arranged package, fly-drive and specialist holidays, as well as organising more bespoke packages.
- Liaised with tour operators to broker best value deals and devise unique upgrade offerings, extending customer choice.
- Organised specialist holidays for 'niche' audiences, including golf, cooking and yoga, which extended the travel season.
- Handled traveller emergencies, including hospitalisations, erupting volcanos and lost passports, liaising with the local consulate, family members and quickly organising alternative arrangements with the hotel and travel companies.

Travel Assistant　　Ultimate Holiday Company　　2012–2014

These were the market leaders in leisure travel, and I was fortunate to receive excellent in-house training in all aspects of being a travel agent.
- Organising travel arrangements for leisure customers.
- Chasing up and checking tickets, schedules and documentation requirements.
- Creating bespoke packages in line with customer preferences.

Education and training
- BTEC National Diploma in Travel and Tourism.
- Training in customer service, sales and influencing.

Interests
- Travel, learning Italian, weight lifting.

CV 3: Functional CV (for a candidate who has taken a career detour into Health and Safety and wants to return to Training)

Gillian Knight

Lampshire, HM1
Mobile: 07983 999999
Email: gknight@googlemail.com

Learning and Development professional, qualified in CIPD and NEBOSH, focused on delivering employee development that significantly enhances employee performance, fosters career agility and reduces organisational risks. This includes creating management and soft skills training, as well as the health and safety courses that were so business-critical during the Covid-19 pandemic. As a trained coach with excellent communication skills, I excel in facilitating learner conversations and creating impactful learning content, as well as conducting training needs diagnostics to establish the real learning need and best mode of delivery. Adept at using learning management systems and evaluating outcomes to track return on investment.

Relevant experience history

Training design

- Successfully identified skills gaps and performance improvement opportunities through consultations with 30+ stakeholders, facilitation of three focus groups, and analysis of pulse surveys. Resulted in the implementation of a more blended learning approach, leading to a 10% increase in learner participation.
- Collaborated closely with external specialists to create tailored compliance training modules specific to our company, enabling much more successful transfer of learning into the workplace, as shown by end of year assessments.
- Designed an employee wellbeing campaign, which included training up 30 managers and six internal mental health first aiders, curating e-learning resources and providing signposting to our Employee Assistance Programme (which saw an 8% increase in referrals, helping people to get the support they need).
- Created comprehensive training materials, such as presentations, manuals, video instruction guides, and a WhatsApp learning group to continue conscientiousness about new learning and share experiences and queries.

Training delivery

- Trained coach and a mentor for Graduate and Apprenticeship programmes, guiding and supporting emerging talent in their career journey.
- Expertise in delivering both in-person workshops and virtual training sessions, utilising various interactive tools available in virtual platforms (e.g., whiteboards, surveys, chat functions).
- Successfully onboarded over 50 new employees each year through a combination of e-learning modules, virtual webinars and on-the-job demonstrations.
- Delivered a manual handling course to over 200 staff members, resulting in a significant reduction of up to 35% in injury reports among previously high-risk teams.

Training administration
- Excellent knowledge of learning management systems and how to track the employee learning journey and analyse impact and inclusivity.
- Co-ordinating coaching and mentoring opportunities both internally and externally for Managers and emerging talent. Promoting the service, matching individuals and dealing with queries.
- Organised a Career Development week for 1,000 staff with a programme of activities for employees, including workshops, webinars, coaching and mentoring opportunities as well as networking events.
- Researched and arranged training providers and external courses to meet specific organisational and employee requirements.

Employment history

Health and Safety Officer **Langleys** **April 2020–to date**

This logistics company specialises in goods and freight transportation and employs 500 staff in a high-risk work environment where training is key to workplace safety.
- Created regularly updated learning materials and advice guides for health and safety protocols to be followed during Covid-19 pandemic, including briefing managers on their responsibilities.
- Initiated highly popular virtual wellness sessions to support employee mental health, attracting over 50 participants.
- Co-ordinated training of 10 in-house mental health champions, providing valuable support networks at a challenging time.
- Established home working health and safety policies and implemented an audit process for managers to mitigate risks.
- Collaborated with internal stakeholders and our EAP provider to offer valuable support services to individuals experiencing stress, tracking service uptake and attendance statistics.
- Delivered manual handling courses for all new staff and refresher sessions.

Learning and Development Officer **Twifold** **July 2017–March 2020**

A global manufacturing company with over 1,000 employees located in the UK.
- Organised a career development week for staff with a range of learning and development events.
- Trained over 20 managers in appraisal processes and absence management to help motivate staff, improve performance and attendance.
- Co-facilitated an action learning group for graduate recruits, fostering networking, knowledge sharing and a supportive environment.
- Organised in-house coaching and mentoring programmes, including request matching, provider liaison, scheduling and invoicing.
- Arranged all aspects of a Management away day for 80 participants, offering a range of training opportunities for personalised growth.
- Tracked and monitored learning activities, feedback and outcomes to optimise training effectiveness and ensure efficient use of resources.

Qualifications

CIPD Certificate in Training Practice		2019
Nebosh H&S Certificate IOSH		2021
BA (Hons) in American Studies (2:ii)	Lincoln University	2017

IN A NUTSHELL

Functional CVs can be a highly effective way of demonstrating your suitability for a particular role or employer, particularly when you may not be an obvious candidate.

Use when:

- you need extra versatility in the structure of your CV
- your last few roles/employers are not as relevant to the job being sought
- your career path has been more haphazard than steady progression
- your employment looks inconsistent, with gaps or lots of short-term roles and you want to play down any work history that could be seen as a distraction
- changing career direction to display your transferable skills
- you want a direct way to show the employer how you meet their competency requirements by choosing particular headings for your CV
- you have worked for one employer for most of your career and you want to demonstrate your versatility on the first page rather than emphasise your limited wider experience
- you want to use paid and unpaid work experience to support your application.

Don't use when:

- applying for a role that is directly compatible with your previous roles
- you can show a history of career progression within related roles.

10 ONE-PAGE CVs

Normally your CV should be no longer than two pages long, or sometimes longer if you are an academic and need to include details of research and publications, etc. However, there are occasions on which a one-page CV could be the best option.

This chapter will help you:

- understand when you may want to use a one-page CV
- write your CV in this format.

First a warning: do not send a one-page CV as part of an application for an advertised job unless you have been specifically requested to do so. The two-page format is the default standard.

However, a one-page CV can work well if you are straight out of school and/or are more limited in the content you can include. You could also use this format for a speculative approach to an employer you are interested in working with. By carefully cherry-picking certain key skills, knowledge or achievements, which you know will appeal to them, you can hook their interest and downplay other things on your regular CV that might be considered more of a distraction.

A one-page CV can also work well if you are self-employed or if your company supplies potential customers with a career background on their staff as part of the company's sales pitch. This is particularly relevant for professional service providers, consultancies or any other enterprise where the individual's expertise is a key factor in winning new customers to the company, e.g. a training specialist.

The great advantage of this CV format is that you don't need to include all of your past employment details. You can refer indirectly to your career history — for example, 'five years working as key account manager for a well-known household brand'. This can be useful if the details of your employment history are either not helpful or if confidentiality is important. If you are approaching a competitor, you may want to be discreet.

PROS AND CONS OF ONE-PAGE CVs

Advantages of a one-page CV

- Can be used as a bio by your employer in your current role, on social media or other PR and personal branding.

- Works well for speculative approaches to employers as a more direct sales pitch.

- Ideal for the self-employed, consultants or career changers who want to emphasise their skills and credentials rather than career history.

Disadvantages of a one-page CV

- Employers will normally expect at least a two-page CV, unless you are straight out of school.

- Recruitment software is likely to rank it less highly than other CVs because there is less content and fewer keywords.

- The balance of information can be tricky to get right, as any claims you make about your skills and experience still need to be substantiated.

On the following pages are a template CV and a specimen CV which you can use as a guide to write your own CV in this format.

Template for a one-page CV

Name
Location (optional)
Mobile:
Email:

Profile (optional)
- Describe yourself in terms of your experience and specialisms. You could include key brand names, organisations worked with or impressive projects.

Key skills and experience or key achievements
- Focus on activities that you have undertaken and that have added value to the organisation, e.g. increased profitability, efficiency, quality.
- Quantify all achievements: use numbers, percentage points, budget size, etc.
- Relate all skills and experience directly to customer's/employer's anticipated needs.

Career history
- Present this in summary form, e.g.:
- 2022 to date: Charity Fundraiser, AJP
- 2018–2022: Funding Project Officer, XYZ
- 2016–2018: Campaign Executive, UKR
- Alternatively your career history can be written in full sentences without naming organisations, e.g. 'Seven years' experience of working with FTSE 100 companies or leading international charities.'

Education/training
Give your highest qualifications and only relevant training.

Affiliations, professional memberships
Include any details that enhance your professional status and/or are prestigious in themselves.

CV 4: One-page CV

Louis Alexander

Liverpool, L14
Mobile: 07777 555555
Email: lm@gmail.com

Career profile
Business transformation specialist with over 15 years of experience devising business strategies for growth, organisational resilience and profitability. Proven track record of successfully turning around underperforming companies and improving financial performance and sustainability. Deep Expertise in Power B1, statistical modelling and Blueprint Facilitation, as well as Stakeholder Management, Process Design and Six Sigma. Wide business experience across many different industries bringing a rigorous analytical approach, commercial acumen and project management capabilities.

Employment history

Business Transformation Consultant   Alpha Change Consultancy   2020–present
- Advising SME clients on business transformation, providing strategic guidance, future-proofing and driving operational improvements. This included delivering savings of £20 million within two years for one firm by creating a more cost-effective business model and reducing financial risk.

Business Analyst   Big Four Professional Services Firm   2015–2020
- Provided business analysis expertise, tracking performance, identifying improvement opportunities and delivering recommendations. Examples include saving circa £250k per year for a charity through reviewing commercial contracts; introducing new management systems for a logistics firm, which enabled more accurate real-time management reporting; and developing a new outsourcing model for a Local Authority facing a budget deficit.

Business Analyst   Global Fashion Brand   2012–2015
- Increased positive customer feedback by 10% and drove a 15% rise in profits by Year 2, by tracking user experience and sales interactions and using the data to devise a new e-commerce hub and customer loyalty scheme. Provided all of the financial modelling and business analytics to incentivise customer spend and referrals.

Education and qualifications
Association of Chartered Certified Accountants (ACCA)   Qualified 2015
BSc (Hons) Accounting   Edmonds University   2010–2013

IN A NUTSHELL

Use a one-page CV when:

- you are self-employed, to use alongside other company marketing material
- it is required by your own organisation as information for their customers
- you wish to upload your CV as a social media profile
- it is specifically requested
- writing a speculative letter to an employer and attaching a CV.

Don't use a one-page CV when:

- you are applying for jobs advertised by an employer or agency as they will expect a chronological or functional CV
- you have good career progression in a related field
- you cannot sprinkle brand names, prestigious companies, projects or substantial money-making achievements in the CV to give it weight.

11 DEVELOPING YOUR OWN CV WEBSITE

It is now relatively easy to set up a website at low cost, and for freelancers and those who work in creative fields, there are many advantages.

This chapter will help you:

- understand whether you should have a CV website
- know what to include on the website.

If you have a portfolio of work that prospective employers would find helpful to view, then consider creating your own website. You can use it to display all of your relevant information and background with examples of your work and testimonials from satisfied clients or employers. This approach is highly suitable for individuals in fields such as:

- designers, artists, performers, journalists, film-makers
- event managers, PR specialists, advertising consultants
- website or game developers
- other freelancers where customers are buying the services of the business owner.

You can include a link to your website within a traditional CV that you send as normal to an employer or to a recruitment website. You can also include it on your LinkedIn profile and business cards.

PROS AND CONS OF HAVING YOUR OWN CV WEBSITE

Advantages of a CV website

- You have complete control of how you promote yourself.
- It can represent your personal brand with far more personality than a standard CV.
- You can show a multi-media portfolio of your work, including images, articles, video and audio.

Disadvantages of a CV website

- You still need a regular CV to apply for jobs on recruitment sites.
- Needs time, commitment and flair to create a site that represents you persuasively.
- The costs of the build and ongoing maintenance costs, including rectifying any technical issues.

How to create your own website

If you are interested in setting up your own website, then, depending on your ambitions, you can either build one yourself if you have the technical skill, hire a website builder to do it for you – although that can cost anywhere from a couple of hundred pounds to many thousands – or use one of the ready-made templates that are available from a host of different sites. Remember, there will also be additional costs to register the site under your chosen name and on the platform that you wish it to be hosted on.

What to include on your website

If you are using your website to obtain your next role or engagement, then it needs to pay as much attention as a regular CV to your key selling points and what you think the target audience is looking for. The visual presentation may be more sophisticated, but there is still no margin for error. Poor layout, spelling mistakes, etc. will not be forgiven.

The website should include:

- your name and contact details
- your credentials, e.g. technical skills, relevant qualifications, education
- what you can offer (do a full sales pitch!)
- information to impress, e.g. exhibitions, prestige projects, well-known customers
- relevant work history (dates optional)
- business-appropriate photo of you (this is much more acceptable on a website than on your CV)
- portfolio of your work, e.g. designs, photos, articles
- video or sound clips, if appropriate
- quotes, testimonials, glowing reviews or case studies.

A website also gives you the chance to express more personal information, perhaps about your approach to your work, e.g. 'My designs are informed by my love of nature', and then explain your philosophy. You can include examples of your work, with the design brief and its impact. You could also include some video of yourself talking about your work or some video testimonials from happy clients.

However, unless you want to go down the influencer route or you are an artist whose background is an important element of their work, then avoid sharing too much personal information. Focus on your work, your professional capabilities and keep it upbeat.

On the following page is an example of a website for a consultancy service. You can find many more examples online, which you can borrow ideas from. It is extremely useful to see what others have developed and what you think works and what doesn't. You can then start to devise your own.

A consultancy service's website

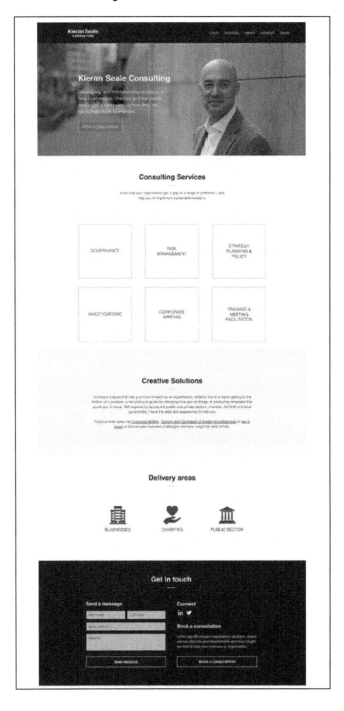

IN A NUTSHELL

- If you normally need to show a portfolio of work to customers or potential employers, you should also have your own website.
- Remember this is a sales pitch, so focus on what you want to sell and what your target audience wants.
- Do not include irrelevant personal information – keep it businesslike.
- Ensure the site is maintained and updated.
- Be realistic on budget and stick to it, as it is very easy to overspend.
- Visually it must look attractive and be error-free.
- Ensure it is easy to contact you.
- Include link to website either within a regular CV, on your LinkedIn profile and on any business cards.

12 MAKING YOUR CV LOOK GOOD

Employers will judge your professionalism not only by the content of your CV but also by the standard of its presentation.

This chapter will help you:

- produce a CV that is visually attractive as well as functional
- decide whether to send a photo
- quality-check your CV so that it is error free.

A nicely presented CV says to the recruiter that you have taken care in your application, and therefore you are likely to:

- want the job because you have clearly made an effort
- have good quality standards because of your attention to detail
- act as a good representative for the company because you understand how to make a good impression.

Your CV will need to be produced using a computer – so if you're not confident in your IT skills, ask someone who is to help you out, or check out **nationalcareers.service.gov.uk** for information on free learning courses, including digital skills. There are also some libraries and charities that can provide access to equipment if you don't have your own.

However, if you are really struggling with the IT demands of writing a CV, then ask someone else if they can type it for you as a favour, or pay to have it done professionally through a local secretarial service or CV service. Then, go and get yourself on a course.

Making your CV look attractive

There are lots of CV templates available on the internet that can make your CV look fantastic visually, with different designs, fonts and even infographics. These can work well if you are saving it as a PDF and sending it by email to a particular individual, or if you are uploading it as an image to your LinkedIn or other online profile.

However, many of those designs do not work well if you are uploading it to a recruitment website. The unusual formatting interferes with the recruitment software's ability to 'parse' or process the content. This means that your information may be only partially stored or even corrupted on the recruitment database, making it less likely you will be found by recruiters using keyword searches to find suitable candidates. This is also why recruitment sites will often encourage you to use their own online CV format, because they know the content you input will be easily 'parsed'.

Here are some guidelines to ensure that your CV looks professional while remaining functional.

> **BEAUTIFY YOUR CV**
>
> - **Compatibility:** avoid columns, shading, boxes, images or infographics etc. as these can interfere with recruitment software.
>
> - **Font size:** choose one standard font throughout, e.g. Calibri size 10–11 pt, with a bigger size for headings.
>
> - **Margins:** use margins of at least 2.5cm on either side and on the top and bottom of the page.
>
> - **Bullet points:** use a standard bullet point format as unusual symbols can confuse software.
>
> - **Punctuation:** be consistent in the use of full stops at the end of bullet points and/or paragraphs.
>
> - **Headings:** use a consistent style for headings, either bold, all capitals and/or slightly bigger font. Underlining tends to looks messy.
>
> - **Alignment:** all headings and paragraphs should be in line with each other, and the text should be aligned to the left rather than justified.
>
> - **White space:** ensure that around headings and paragraphs there is plenty of white space to make it easier to read.
>
> - **Length:** normally no longer than two A4 pages, unless you are an academic or are listing projects.
>
> - **Colour:** black and white always works, but you can use colour if you ensure all words are easily readable.

If you are in a creative profession, then your CV is also a chance to show your originality and style. Create one version that is distinctively unique, and you can either send this as a PDF directly to individuals or load it as an image on your website. However, you will also need a more traditional version for platforms using recruitment software. (See page 153 for more information on CVs for creative professionals.)

Say 'cheese!'

In certain countries it is standard procedure to send a photo with your CV. However, in the UK, strong anti-discrimination legislation means that photos are not encouraged on CVs because they can potentially leave the employer open to accusations of bias. This is also why some bigger companies adopt a 'blind CVs' policy, stripping the name and other personal information from CVs so that recruiters can focus on capabilities alone.

However, if an employer does request a photo – perhaps because the role is entertainment-related or their recruitment function is handled abroad – then include one, but make sure it is appropriate for the role rather than a holiday snap.

Quality control

The odd spelling error in everyday email communication is forgivable – but when you are job-hunting, it becomes a reason to place you on the reject pile. In a survey by Personal Career Management, nine out of ten CVs had errors on them. These included spelling, grammatical and formatting errors that would easily have been spotted by a proper read through.

Does this matter? Well, 58% of employers in south-east UK who were asked, said that they would reject applicants who made such mistakes. So why is it so common to see spelling mistakes? There may be a number of reasons.

- It's not always easy to pick up spelling mistakes on a computer screen.
- Spell-checkers don't pick up every misspelling, particularly if the misspelt word is a valid word in its own right or is okay in American English.
- Spelling and grammar is a weak point for many people, including people with dyslexia, and therefore more challenging to get right.

Despite this, employers who may be sympathetic to the above will also consider that it shows a certain sloppiness when there are so many tools that can help you get it right, including:

- the grammar and spell-check facility on your computer or available on the internet
- copying the content into ChatGPT or another AI prompt and asking it to improve the writing and grammar
- asking someone else to check it for you – they almost always spot the mistakes!

IN A NUTSHELL

The way your CV looks is as important as the content. Make sure you:

- avoid a feature-heavy layout, unless sending as a PDF
- take time to make the layout look professional
- do not include a photo unless specifically requested
- check, double-check and triple-check spellings.

13 CVs FOR SPECIFIC CAREER CHALLENGES

Everyone has a different career situation with their own unique challenges. This chapter features CV advice for those in the following groups:

- graduates and school-leavers
- career changers
- people with career gaps
- technical professionals
- creative and media
- managers and executives
- internal promotions.

The basic principles of CV writing apply no matter what your personal situation. Research the job, demonstrate you have what they are looking for and then organise the information on the page in an attractive and professional manner.

This chapter offers additional tips for where organising and presenting the content presents its own challenges.

CVs for graduates and school-leavers

Looking for your first 'proper' job is exciting and daunting. How do you convince an employer you are a great person to hire, when you have limited work experience to draw on?

Well, everyone has to start somewhere. What employers are looking for in their young staff is potential: the capacity to learn, the motivation to work hard and the ability to get on with people. They also want to see that you have thought about why you are suitable for the role and that you genuinely want to do it.

So, let's look at how your CV can help convince them that you have got what it takes.

Career objective/career profile

If you are using your CV for a specific role, include a career objective that states you are looking exactly for that role. For example, a graduate with experience of working Saturdays with an electrical retail store might apply for a sales-type role with this career profile:

> 'Business graduate experienced in retail sales and customer service environments. Used to advising customers on a range of complex technical products, processing sales and helping with merchandising. Regularly earned bonuses as a result of meeting personal and team targets. Looking for a position where I can further my interest in sales and business development.'

However, if they wanted to apply for an accountancy role then they could try:

'Business graduate seeking trainee accountancy role to further my interest in the financial aspects of running a business. Used to dealing with cost calculations, payment processes and following strict financial procedures as a result of my experience working for large electrical retailer.'

Academic studies

You may want to put this as one of your first headings so that they can see you are a new job-hunter.

Include details about the components of your university or college course only if it is directly relevant to the job sought, e.g. you have a marketing degree and are applying for a marketing-related role, or your course in social care has given you an understanding of the community roles you are interested in.

You may also want to highlight how your course required you to learn and demonstrate any of the following highly transferable professional skills:

- capturing data, analysing and interpreting information
- IT skills and any software packages used
- team-working, group project work and collaboration
- communication and presentation skills
- research and report writing
- creativity, initiative and design ability.

If your courses were completed abroad, indicate the level to which they are equivalent, e.g. Baccalauréat (the A level equivalent). Some graduate-entry programmes will require you to have a minimum grade on your degree. This is usually a non-negotiable requirement, and if you don't meet the employer's specific requirements then you might as well not apply. However, if you are intent on working for that particular organisation, you can always look to enter via a different route, i.e. direct entry into one of their other jobs or via an Apprenticeship scheme (these are open to anyone regardless of qualifications; visit **www.gov.uk/apply-apprenticeship** to find out what is available).

Relevant work experience

Young people by definition have less work experience, so you have to make the most of what you have — whether it was paid or unpaid. It doesn't matter how long you worked in each role, nor the job title; it is the transferable skills you acquired that are most important, e.g.:

- Covid-19 NHS helper: team working and conscientiousness
- administrative work: accurate data entry
- working in a shop: customer service skills
- catering work: health and safety awareness
- helping at an event: dealing with the general public
- factory work: team work
- telesales: working to targets.

For instance if you have worked in the following temporary roles you can talk about what the experience helped you learn.

TABLE 11: SKILLS GAINED FROM TEMPORARY ROLES

Customer service	Retail	Courier services
Communication skills	Selling	Organisational skills
Working to targets	Merchandising	Efficiency
Following processes	Inventory management	Working under pressure
Information gathering	Policies and processes	Using technology
Using a CRM database	Product knowledge	Time management
Resilience	Point of sale systems	Attention to detail
Conflict handling	Dealing with customers	Stamina
Emotional intelligence	Team working	Reliability
Patience and empathy	Problem solving	Problem solving
Multi-tasking	Working to targets	Quality control
Positive attitude	Influencing	Brand ambassador

Voluntary work activities: these show your community spirit, energy, work ethic as well as potentially transferable skills, e.g.:

- conservation activities: team spirit and sense of purpose
- leading a charity bike ride: people management and logistics
- creating a gaming society: recruiting and organising people
- raising money for a good cause: influencing and persuading
- writing blogs for a youth group newsletter: written communication skills.

> ### USING AI TO HELP YOU
>
> - Using the Chat function, ask: *What skills and knowledge might I have learnt from working in a role in ... (insert job title)? How could I write this in a way that would work on my CV?*
> - The AI will give you some very helpful ideas. However, remember that you need to always personalise these to ensure they are genuine.

Additional information

Positions of responsibility: include examples where you have taken charge of a task, shown leadership or other skills, e.g.:

- activities with the National Citizen Service or Duke of Edinburgh scheme
- student helpline volunteer or mentor
- course representative
- guide/scout leader/air cadet
- community responsibilities, e.g. church, youth groups.

Also include any other activities that show your capabilities, e.g.:

- sports achievements and memberships
- any design projects
- any entrepreneurial activity, e.g. selling merchandise
- public speaking/debating society
- amateur dramatics/music activities.

Relevant skills: you should itemise any specific skills you have that may be relevant, e.g.:

- your IT skills and capabilities, e.g. advanced user of Word
- specific communication skills, e.g. writing, presenting
- language skills
- first aid
- coaching
- clean driving licence.

Interests: it can be helpful for a young job-seeker to put down their hobbies and interests. Make sure these are genuine and show you in a good light, as you are likely to be asked about them.

Referees

Two referees are the norm, one academic and one either work-related, or possibly a character reference from someone respected in the community who knows you. Do not include these on your CV, but have them ready to give the employer following the interview.

Graduate CV example

Opposite is the CV of someone whose experience in her target industry is relatively limited – just two work placements of a couple of weeks each. However, she has used these to their full potential and strengthened her case by including the transferable skills she obtained from the part-time and temporary jobs she worked in while she was a student.

CV 5: Recent graduate CV

Sian Forrester

sian@gmail.com
Tel: 07770 555555
Forreston, SV5

Career profile
Recent graduate in Business Management and Marketing, with experience of working for a leading creative media agency and in customer-focused, commercially driven businesses. Articulate, numerate and a fast learner, I'm keen to combine my business studies with the practical insights I've gained from working directly with customers, to help companies create and enhance their brands. Excellent IT skills, including Word, Excel, PowerPoint, Canva and Google analytics.

Relevant skills and experience
- BSc (Hons) 2:1 in Business Management and Marketing with modules on Brand Management, Analytics, Innovation, Consumer Psychology and Management modules on Finance, People Management, Strategy, Legal and Technology.
- Internship with Deft Creative Agency where I worked with the campaign planning team on two different projects including the launch of a new health food brand and a brand refresh for a retail company.
- Awarded a Distinction by a panel of industry professionals for my student presentation on an advertising campaign for a drinks brand.
- Dissertation on the impact of influencers which included researching the perceived and actual impact of an influencer-led campaign.
- Excellent business management knowledge and skills, including completing modules on financial operations, cost control and forecasting.
- Superb communication skills and customer focus, developed both from my graduate course where I had to produce reports and give presentations, but also from roles I've undertaken in sales and customer service where I've had to understand customers' needs, sell appropriate solutions and resolve issues.
- Positive attitude and eagerness to learn. As a recent graduate, I know there is lots to learn but I have always been a fast and keen learner, teaching myself software programs such as Canva, developing my listening skills as a volunteer for the Student Nightline and actively keeping updated about market and societal trends.

Education

BSc (Hons) 2:i, Business Management and Marketing   Cartell University   2020–2023
3 A Levels: English (B), Economics (B), French (C)   2019
6 GCSEs with Level 7 in English Language and all others above Level 5

Work experience

Placement   **Deft Creative Agency**   **2022 and 2023**

First worked for Deft in 2022, but they then invited me back for 2023. My activities included:
- Helping compile competitor research for a client to be used in a strategy discussion
- Verifying facts for a pitch to a prospective corporate client
- Supporting the social media campaign for a client and feeding back on its impact
- Providing a shortlist of influencers for consideration by a client
- Liaising with the art directors and copy writers to schedule discussion meetings
- Working with accounts to understand and check client billing records
- Supporting the planning team in organising an email campaign to over 10,000 businesses.

Customer Service Assistant   **123 Ltd**   **January 2021–present**

Worked as a customer assistant for this energy utilities firm during my studies. This involved:
- Meeting the monthly sales targets for client conversions through cold-calling leads
- Ensuring all information shared was accurate and compliant with strict regulatory procedures
- Resiliently and diplomatically handling callers who were sometimes unhappy about being approached
- Communicating clearly with customers from very different backgrounds
- Using a CRM system and producing end of day reports to track outputs and successes.

Sales Assistant   **Grant Shoes**   **February 2019–January 2020**

Worked as sales assistant in a high street shoe shop. This included:
- Keeping waiting times low by assisting customers quickly and efficiently
- Processing payments for purchases and notifying the manager of any payment issues
- Helping organise the stockroom to make it easier to find required shoes
- Increasing customer spend by recommending shoe accessories
- Assisting with store security to ensure stock was protected from potential theft or damage
- Working to group weekly sales targets.

Additional information
- Volunteer for the Nightline Student Helpline
- Helped run social media campaign to encourage student participation in elections
- Regular contributor to online forum for film buffs
- French language skills.

CVs for career changers

If you are looking to change your career, you need to be canny about how you market yourself on your CV. You are not going to be an obvious candidate when recruiters look at your employment history, so you'll need to grab the employer's attention early on to convince them of your suitability and commitment.

Let's look at some of the practical tips that will help you.

Functional CV format
- Use a CV in the functional format to highlight your transferable skills and experience.
- Show on the first page how you meet the competencies required on the job description/person specification form.
- Include on the first page all experiences, including paid, extra-curricular or voluntary work, that are directly relevant to the role.
- Employment history with dates and job titles should go on the second page.

Training
Some roles will require you to have undertaken specific training or have other credentials. If you have these, then include them on the first page. If you haven't, then research what training you need, and show in your CV that you are either currently undertaking it or due to enrol on a course. However, don't expect a new employer to pay for your training.

Considered decision
- Show that you know what the work realistically involves by talking about how you've spent time shadowing someone in the role, talked with people in the field, or about other research you have undertaken. By including this, you demonstrate that your decision to change career has been well thought through rather than a whim.
- Explain in your career profile why you should be chosen for the role in question, i.e. how you meet their requirements, but also what you have to offer that is over and above the conventional candidate.
- Use key buzzwords from the industry. Showing awareness of the industry's trends, specialist knowledge, etc. will help position you as an 'insider' rather than a 'wannabe'.

Career changer CV example

Opposite is an example of a CV of an operational Team Leader who wants to move into HR. He highlights his relevant knowledge and experience on the first page and states a commitment to undertaking professional training. He also shows that he was a high achiever in a previous role with very transferable skills.

CV 6: Career change CV

Callum Gabel

Email: cg@gmail.com
Tel: 07888 555666
Mardenham RL23

Career profile
Highly skilled, Human Resources-focused people manager with 5+ years' experience helping teams navigate intense change, including the response to the Covid-19 pandemic and a company restructuring. HR-related experience includes redesigning work processes and roles, assisting with recruitment campaigns and staff training, and being an active member of the Wellbeing and Diversity and Inclusion staff forums. I have always worked very closely with HR to ensure compliance with employment law, policies and best practice, and am furthering my knowledge with a CIPD Certificate which I will complete this year. I'm seeking an HR business partner role, where my strong operational experience will be an asset in supporting the HR requirements of front-line managers.

Relevant skills and experience

Employee relations
- Handled restructuring discussions with team, including exiting one staff member through redundancy. This involved ensuring all legal and contractual issues were handled appropriately, and motivating the remaining staff for the transition.
- Fully trained in disciplinary and grievance handling, having attended both in-house training and external management courses. Worked closely with HR on a performance capability and a gross misconduct issue, both of which needed handling with great sensitivity to avoid any legal claims and achieve a clean exit.
- Supported the wellbeing of team members and colleagues as a trained internal Wellbeing Champion and Mental Health First Aider, buddying three individuals in the last year and throughout the Covid-19 pandemic.

Recruitment and selection
- Fully trained in recruitment and selection best practice and the relevant employment law.
- Designed four new roles following organisational restructuring, determining key competencies, shortlisting and interviewing candidates and handling all salary and contract negotiations.
- Liaised with agencies, job centres and apprenticeship providers to recruit and develop talent pipelines.

Performance management
- My team has been identified as one of the 'high-performing' teams in the organisation and held up by the CEO as a model of excellence.
- Conduct performance reviews with four team members per year, plus monthly individual and team meetings. Determine team and individual bonuses against business and personal targets.
- Mentor to two graduate trainees, both of whom are now on the internal fast-track programme.

Training and development
- Identified key competencies and behaviours required from team through conducting a work flow analysis, identifying current skills and areas for development. As a result, the onboarding programme was re-focused and training refresher activities introduced.
- Set group training targets to bridge areas of gap. One early result is an acceleration of customer response time by 15% and greater team versatility for contingencies.
- Organised a series of formal and informal training solutions, ranging from bite-sized webinars and workshops to coaching and work shadowing.

Career history

2019–present   Service Manager   BRG Holdings

Joined this fast-paced technology organisation as a graduate trainee and was quickly promoted to manager, managing a team of four reports in a division generating £50 million+ per year.
- Improved team productivity by 15% by streamlining processes and reconfiguring roles.
- Appointed project team leader on a new Customer Service initiative, rolling out key messages and embedding new behaviours. As a result, customer evaluations improved by 25%.
- Key liaison person for new £10 million service-level agreement, smoothing some early difficulties and now delivering efficiently with substantial cost savings.
- Built new relationships with leading players in our industry, such as Jason White Group and Dales Consultants, which have evolved into new joint ventures worth £2 million per year.
- Reduced absence by 20% in my department as a result of tackling and resolving a particularly sensitive health issue that previously no-one had been willing to address.
- Active member of the Staff Wellbeing Committee and the Diversity and Inclusivity Network, helping to shape the agenda, policies and the provision of support for those in need.

Education

BA American Studies	Cartell University	2016–2019
CIPD, CPP	Central University	Due to complete September 2024

Training

2-day Coaching Course	Recruitment and Selection	Objective Setting
Disciplinary and Grievance	Appraisal Training	Influencing Skills
1st-line Management Course	Managing Absence	Handling Conflict

CVs for people with career gaps

Few people have worked continuously from their first job to retirement, and most people will have gaps somewhere in their career for all kinds of reasons, including:

- raising a family
- resigning and then looking for a new role
- redundancy or dismissal
- caring for a relative or other dependant
- ill-health or an accident
- taking a course or travelling
- taking some time out for other reasons.

However, employers can be quite suspicious of career gaps and, depending on the length and frequency of the gaps, will want to be reassured that there is no hidden problem.

How do you deal with this?

Date format
Where the gap is only a few months, you can use the month to month or even year to year format for employment dates, e.g. February 2022–January 2023 (for gaps of a few weeks either end) and 2022–2023 (for gaps of a few months). You could even group together a few different past employments, e.g. '2021–2023: During this time, undertook varied administrative roles for organisations such as Jackson Foods and Dales Consultants in the telecommunications and retail sector.'

Functional CV format
Use this CV format to highlight on the first page all of your key skills and experience. Put all past employer details and dates on the second page, which will serve to downplay their importance.

Give a positive explanation
If the gaps are still noticeable you may need to give an explanation, especially if you are completing an online CV form that insists you give reasons for leaving each role. It is fine to explain that your career break was for family reasons

if you were raising a family or looking after a relative. Equally, if you were travelling, studying or on an interesting adventure, then these are also fine to state.

Employers are going to be extremely understanding about career turbulence during the Covid-19 pandemic, as so many people lost their jobs, had to change career or were unable to work because they were shielding for themselves or others.

If you do have a longish career gap, it's important that you find a positive way to describe what you were doing at that time, rather than saying 'unemployed'.

Talk about any voluntary work you were undertaking: supporting neighbours during the pandemic, home-schooling, studying, writing, helping out with a friend's business, or working with a career coach to decide on your next move. Present an active, positive image of someone who may not have been in paid employment, but who was pursuing activities that added to their employability.

If the reason for the gap is a negative one, such as illness or an accident, then include this as an explanation on an online CV form only as a last resort. Any mention of poor health on your CV, even if it was a long time ago, will raise concerns over your fitness to work. Where you do mention it, phrase the wording to make it clear that whatever medical problem there was, it is now fully resolved or manageable, e.g. 'Unable to work as broke my foot in accident. Now fully recovered.'

If there is an ongoing health issue that may affect your ability to work, or you are an ex-offender, see Chapter 1 for more information on how to handle these with an employer.

Prove you are ready to work

If you are looking to return to work after a career gap, then you will need to demonstrate to the employer that you have kept your skills fresh during your time away, that you are up to date, up to speed and willing and ready for the challenges of a full working life.

This could include:

- running your own small business
- helping out at a family/friend's business
- taking a refresher or 'return to work' course in your field, e.g. teaching, nursing
- voluntary work
- work placements or mature apprenticeships
- re-training for a new career direction.

You will also need good IT skills. So, if you have been away for a while, an IT course should probably be your first port of call.

Career gap CV example

The following CV is an example of someone wishing to return to paid employment following parental leave. They want to change career direction and work in education rather than go back into their original field of market research. They have undertaken voluntary work at the local school to gain relevant experience and to check whether this is something that they enjoy. They have also taken advantage of every training course available at the school, and see a role as a classroom assistant as the means to a new career in education.

CV 7: Returning to work following parental leave and wanting to change career direction

Pat Jones

Middletown, BC5
Mobile: 07898 555555
Email: pjones@gmail.co.uk

Career profile

Classroom assistant with experience of working with children in educational and informal settings at school and in the community. DBS-checked and trained in first aid. Have attended workshops on how to deal with children with special needs, and used this training to assist pupils with mobility and learning challenges. Excellent numeracy and written skills gained from my previous market research background. Strong IT skills, including Microsoft Word, Excel, PowerPoint and a range of educational technologies. I enjoy helping children develop their potential and build their confidence, especially those who find school challenging. Due to attend classroom assistant training in January 2024.

Relevant skills and experience

- Knowledge and experience of classroom work through working as a teacher's helper for Reception and Year 1 at local primary school.
- Assisted a teacher in Year 1 by supporting a child with learning challenges, which enabled them to participate in classroom learning.
- Supported primary school children with their reading and helped in the library, encouraging the children to have fun with books.
- Took care of the younger children in helping them with their lunch, playground supervision, etc.
- Supervised the children in the cookery class, helping them learn about healthy eating and making snacks to take home.
- Have attended courses in health and safety, diversity and child protection.
- Involved in running of local toddler group, including preparation for an inspection, which was highly praised for the excellent resources, organisation and safety standards.
- Highly IT literate enabling me to help pupils develop their computer skills, using educational technology and resources, such as interactive whiteboards.
- Versatile communication skills developed through previous experience as a market researcher, which required excellent facilitation skills and the ability to talk with people from very different backgrounds.

Work experience

Classroom helper   Hays School, Gorton   2023–present

- Supporting the teacher within the classroom by helping individual children with work activities.
- Administrative duties, e.g. photocopying, making teachers' resources, checking paperwork.
- Assisting a special needs child with mobility challenges to participate in school life.
- Provided extra support on school visits to places such as the village library, a farm and the local museum.
- Helping the children look after the school garden, sowing seeds and watering plants.

Career break   2020–2023

During this time, I was involved in:
- organising school events (PTA committee member)
- helping run a voluntary community toddler playgroup that achieved superb feedback following an inspection
- administrative work for the family business, including typing correspondence, spreadsheets, etc.
- freelance market research project work.

Market researcher   Jason White Group   2013–2020

- Devising and leading market research campaigns via customer focus groups, one-to-one interviews and street surveys.
- Designing and evaluating questionnaires to meet the client's objectives.
- Analysing information and producing statistical reports to enable clients to make informed decisions.
- Supervising and inducting other market researchers.
- Ensuring quality control through all aspects of the market research process.

Education and qualifications

BA History (2:i)   University of Greaterhampton   1999–2003

Three A levels: History (B), Geography (B) Economics (C); eight GCSEs, including English and Maths.

IT skills

Excellent Word, Excel and PowerPoint Skills. Also experienced in working with a number of different databases to input data and produce detailed reports.

Interests

Reading, swimming and genealogy.

Technical CVs

When an employer is looking for a candidate with specific technical skills, your first priority is to demonstrate you have the particular expertise they are looking for. Without this, your CV will not be considered.

However, given that your CV may well be viewed first by a non-technical person who is responsible for initial shortlisting, it's crucial that you write about your expertise in a way that makes it easy for them to see your suitability.

Remember that in addition to your expertise, you need to present an image of a candidate who has all the desirable personality behaviours, e.g. good communication skills, conscientiousness, etc. See Chapter 4 for a reminder.

Let's look at how you can achieve the balance between the hard technical skills in your CV and the softer skills.

Keywords

Keywords on your CV are essential if recruiters and employers are to find you on their candidate application database. Your CV therefore needs to list all of your technical skills, qualifications and relevant courses for the job within the first half page of your CV or in your profile.

As we saw in Chapter 7, you can usually tell the keywords likely to be used, as they will be in the role job descriptions and person specifications. You can also ask AI what type of keywords it thinks are most likely to be used by recruiters for particular types of roles, and ensure that these are included too.

Repetition

Recruitment software will rank candidates more highly if the keywords it is looking for, or associated words, are mentioned several times in their CV, e.g. if you make several mentions of expertise in Java, the software will assume that this more accurately represents your professional skills than if it's only mentioned once on the second page of your CV.

Years of experience
Include the number of years of experience you have of a particular technology, as recruiters will use keyword search to prioritise candidates, e.g. 'more than five years' experience' or '5+ years' experience'.

CV format
A functional CV format can be useful to prioritise the relevant skills on the first page of your CV. Length of CV is ideally still two pages. However, an experienced developer or researcher could have a longer CV if it lists all of the key projects with which they have been involved. Digital specialists may also consider hosting their own CV website to show off their technical skills in the construction of the site as well as its content.

Bigger picture
Show that you do not operate in an 'expert' ivory tower by always sharing the impact of your work to date. For instance, the impact of a project on the business, community or society, its purpose and any success measures.

Soft skills
Emphasise your communication skills; technical people often neglect to mention these, but they are essential in any job. Include examples of communicating with technical teams and non-technical people, e.g. external consultants, end users, customers and stakeholders. Talk about collaboration, influencing and leading change, creativity, problem-solving and motivating others. Technical CVs can tend to be dry and full of functional detail about programming languages or scientific research, etc., and neglect to give a sense of the individual as someone who is easy to work with and gets things done.

Project work
Regardless of the date order, highlight the projects of most relevance to your target employer. Here's an outline of the things it would be useful for you to include.

- The project size, financial value, number of staff involved or affected.
- What did you do in respect of planning and preparation, information gathering, stakeholder discussions, monitoring, risk assessment, quality control?

- What was the purpose of the project and the resulting impact, either of your particular input or the wider project as a whole?
- Demonstrate your ability to quickly build trusted relationships, establishing rapport and respect with business customers and other staff.
- Show your ability to manage and work with diverse teams of people, including virtual teams if appropriate.
- Include examples of handling challenges, conflicts and setbacks, and how you helped steer things back on course.
- State projects that were completed on schedule, to budget, etc.
- Include positive feedback and favourable quality evaluations.
- Emphasise people and financial management skills, e.g. budgeting, monitoring finances, recruiting and developing staff, etc.

Starting a career in a technical field

You may have attended your course and obtained your technical qualifications but employers will want to see how you have applied your skills. This is of course more of a challenge when you are just starting your career and your experience is limited. If this is the case, consider offering free or low-cost technical services to family, friends, charitable organisations, etc. For instance, if you are a website developer, perhaps you could devise one for your local community group, charity or a friend to enable you to build up a portfolio of your work.

In your CV use an objective statement in your career profile that shows your enthusiasm for this kind of work and your intention to pursue a career in this direction, along with your qualifications and your ability to learn quickly. (See page 114 for CVs for those early in their career.)

Technical CV example

The CV example in this section is of a web-developer with three years' professional experience who is looking to specialise in e-commerce. He specifies the technical skills used for each project, and also demonstrates his understanding that the purpose of his work is to help his client make money through increased sales.

CV 8: Technical CV

Robert Ongwe

Greater Morton, SL1
Mobile: 07777 555555
Email: rongwe@gmail.co.uk
www.robertongwe.com

Career profile

Web-developer with 3+ years' experience building and enhancing e-commerce sites for businesses as diverse as global stationery brands, artisan businesses and training providers. Highly skilled and efficient in creating customer-friendly digital shopping experiences, by using both standard templates and bespoke solutions, including animated features, story-telling approaches and gamification. I enjoy working closely with the client to ensure the site's functionality and aesthetics work in alignment to maximise sales uplift. Excellent technical and program languages skills, with a strong understanding of UI principles.

Key skills

- Languages: HTML, JavaScript, CSS, PHP, Java, ASP.Net, C#, L, DHTML, XML, XSLT
- Technical skills: MySQL, SQL Server, IIS, UNIX/LINUX, Microsoft Visual SourceSafe, SEO

Education

BSc Computer Science (2:i)   University of Crawford   2016–2019
Course included: web technology; computer architecture; Java, software systems; algorithms and data structures; advanced database and operating systems; networks; graphical user interfaces.

Career history

Compuware Consultancy Services   July 2020–present   e-Commerce Web-developer
Digital services consultancy providing a range of IT business solutions.

- Designed and developed bespoke multicurrency e-shop for Bright Greeting Cards using SQL Server and ASP.Net, incorporating payment systems, customer account management, stock control and tracking information. This increased turnover by 25% in the first year.
- Used MySQL to re-vamp payment arrangements for online gaming website using a secure key-based system. Created facility for one-off and subscription payments, loyalty schemes, bonus item codes and referral deals. This increased average customer spend by 15% per visit.
- Integrated a stock control system and Point of Sale (POS) interface to improve sales and delivery information for a rapidly growing artisan food retailer. This helped ease distribution log-jams that had previously caused difficulty.

- Designed bespoke shopping cart design for RST UK, a high-end global fashion retailer using JavaScript. The result was a highly attractive and unique interactive product browsing experience aligned with the customer's luxury brand values.
- Advised customers on search engine optimisation, generating reports using Google Analytics and Hitwise. Extensive liaison with SEO specialists to support marketing campaigns through organic campaigns and pay per click.
- Maintenance of several websites using HTML, CSS, PHP and browser-based content management systems to ensure fully functioning at all times.
- Initiated regular tests to benchmark conversion rates and as a result managed to increase click-through rate by 10% for five clients within the first month of analysis.
- Have initiated extensive research on SEO, including in-depth reading, attendance at related forums, keeping up to date with latest developments in this field.
- Client evaluations have frequently rated my input to be of a high standard, and commented on my helpfulness.

Maytec Solutions   **June 2019–June 2020**   **Web-developer**

London-based IT consultancy offering a range of web-based services to corporate clients predominantly in the creative and media field.
- Experienced in the functional testing of both new and existing sites, usability, accessibility, interface and browser capability.
- Providing maintenance and answering queries from customers regarding existing sites and advising on enhancements.
- Designed and developed web-based survey builder using PHP to interactively create and display surveys online.

Dales   **December 2016–2019**   **Events Assistant**

Worked for this event company throughout my student course.
- Welcoming visitors to exhibition and conference events providing information packs.
- Helping guests with a range of queries, from routine signposting to assisting visitors feeling unwell.
- Directing traffic in the car park to ensure safe parking and exits at busy times.
- Security duties, including helping manage crowds safely, checking tickets and protecting equipment.

Additional information
- Member of British Computing Society (MCBS)
- My online profile: www.robertongwe.com, with links to my website portfolio

Creative CVs

If you are applying for a role as a creative professional or to an organisation that delivers a creative product or service, e.g. a media company, then the aesthetics of your CV and the tone of the content may need a less formal and more contemporary vibe. There are many different creative templates available on the web, so try experimenting with fonts, layouts and even graphics. This CV should be saved as a PDF in order to be easily read and accessed when sent directly to employers via email. However, this type of CV format is not as easily searchable on general recruitment websites. This means that for those sites, you should create an additional CV version in a more traditional format that can be 'parsed' by the database, or complete the site's own online CV builder.

You might also be tempted to do something wacky to grab attention, especially if the competition is intense. Printing your CV on a T-shirt or wearing it as a sandwich board outside their offices might get you noticed, if you're struggling to get shortlisted through conventional means. However, you also need to think about practicalities – can anyone actually read a CV printed on cotton? Also, they are not going to hire you on the gimmick alone; you are still going to need to follow it up with a conventional CV that outlines why you are a great person to hire.

This is why it is so important to focus on the content first and the messages you want to convey. You can then think about the medium that will best carry it for you.

The content
- **Skills and experience:** establish your credibility early on. Prioritise relevant training, academic history and track record.
- **Projects:** include details of your work, including what the brief was, what you had to do to make it happen, its impact and customer feedback.
- **Business-focused:** emphasise your professionalism and business savviness by talking about how you helped win new customers or repeat business, increased the audience size, kept to a tight budget or worked to demanding timelines.
- **Rave reviews:** include any examples where your work has been judged favourably by others, e.g. any awards won, commendations. Don't be modest about your talent.

- **Name-drop:** if you've worked with high-profile people or companies then use their names within your CV to gain kudos by association.
- **Artist statement:** if you are a creative artist, you could also include a short and clear statement of your work and philosophy as an artist, such as the themes in your work. The tone on this can be tricky to get right, so it's helpful to get feedback from others.
- **Enthusiasm:** employers will be looking for a sense of your passion for this type of work, so use lots of positive action words to communicate this. You may even want to include how your work extends into your hobbies, e.g. painting or writing fiction.

The design
- You can use a professional publishing package like Canva or one of the free templates available via Google or Microsoft.
- Experiment with graphics, logos, photos, columns, shapes – these should complement the content not overwhelm it.
- If you're a graphic designer, then try to create a CV with a distinctive visual identity, rather like your own personal branding. Use a theme that works with your LinkedIn profile, business cards, etc., in the same way that you would with a corporate client and their brand identity.
- Including photos or icons to illustrate examples of your work can look great, but be careful not to overcrowd. You can always include links to an online portfolio available via your own website or LinkedIn page.
- Save as a PDF to preserve the format.

> *I worked for a company operating nightclubs, and a candidate sent in his CV in the form of a bottle of Budweiser. He replaced the label with a tiny version of his CV – the bottle was still full – and then sent it through the post to us. It definitely caught the eye and the imagination, but as the CV wasn't readable he wasn't successful in his application.*
>
> Helen Isaac, HR Business Partner

Creative CV example
The following CV is an example of a CV for a graphic designer, where the layout is as important as the content. The designer has personalised it with examples of her work, but they've remembered that, as in any business, it's the substance not just the style that is important.

CV 9: Creative CV for a graphic designer

VISUAL STORYTELLER: TRANSFORMING IDEAS INTO STUNNING VISUALS

Award-winning Graphic Designer, with a superb track record creating distinctive visual branding which conveys both the clients' key messages and the essence of their corporate personality. Excellent knowledge of a range of design tools including Adobe Creative Suite and the new cutting-edge generative software.

EDUCATION

BA Hons 2:1 Graphic Design | London College| graduated 2019

CONTACT ME

- 07767 777 777
- esmith@email.com
- www.esmithdesigns.com
- Northwoods, SP1 8AJ

EMMA SMITH
Graphic designer

KEY SKILLS

Proficient in **Adobe Creative Suite (Photoshop, Illustrator, InDesign) Canva, Html** and **CSS**

Creative ideation: Understanding the brief, researching, brainstorming and concept development, sketching and mood-boards, audience testing and refining

Branding: Experienced in developing and revitalizing brand identities to create a strong and memorable brand presence

Digital Design: Skilled in crafting email marketing templates, and social media graphics that optimize user experience and engagement

Print Media: Expertise in designing marketing collateral, brochures, flyers, posters, and packaging that effectively communicate messages and drive conversions

Typography and Colour Theory: Adept at selecting and customizing fonts and using colour psychology to convey the intended tone and mood of design projects

Communication: Excellent verbal and written communication skills, liaising directly with clients, advising and problem-solving, ensuring they are happy with the results

Time Management: Used to managing multiple projects with challenging deadlines, often requiring versatility and patience when priorities change

GRAPHIC DESIGN EXPERIENCE
The Graphic Design Company | 2019–present

- Won the SE Design Award for my designs for the Grow Organic brand, a new eco-conscious lifestyle business. The design was commended for its avoidance of clichés, its wit and freshness

- Developed poster and social media adverts for launch of a new sportswear line by Play with a distinctive techno vibe designed to appeal to the young adult market. This was so successful that I was commissioned to work on their follow-up campaign for outdoor wear

- Designed logo and corporate branding for the legal firm, Formant and Jones, who had recently undergone a merger and needed a new shared corporate identity. The differing perspectives meant that this project required especially sensitive handling, however, I was able to achieve a consensus with a design that pleased all parties

- Commissioned by Wright Stationery Ltd to produce a digital online brochure product. Using Adobe Design Suite and generative AI tools, I created fun and unusual visuals which made this a lively reading experience rather than just a functional one

- Created exhibition materials for Lido Consultants, including attention-grabbing, pop-up banners and T-shirts for staff, designed to encourage conversation and enhance brand recognition

- Created the visuals for an email marketing campaign for a community charity as part of an appeal for funding and volunteers. This was designed to provoke an emotional response as part of an urgent call to action for more support

- Worked closely with the sales team at AJ Staffing, to create sales literature which reflected the more dynamic customer experience they offered, with fun team profiles and graphics that were fizzing with energy

EXPERTISE

Creativity	✓
Visual Storytelling	✓
Technical Skills	✓
Collaboration	✓
Client Relations	✓

CV advice for managers and executives

Advice for managers
A managerial role is generally one that has responsibilities for planning and directing the work of others and the effective functioning of a particular department or unit. If you are applying for managerial-type roles, then in addition to job-specific information there will be some generic skills and competencies that are likely to be required.

Examples of these include:
- operational experience or subject expertise in the field
- people management, recruiting, developing, motivating and performance-managing staff
- financial and resource management, including commercial acumen
- planning and organising day-to-day work and projects with goal-setting
- problem-solving, resolving conflicts and issues
- implementing change and improvements
- excellent communication skills, emotional intelligence and stress tolerance
- following and enforcing rules and processes.

All of these elements should be reflected in the CV, with practical examples of how you have demonstrated them.

Advice for executives
An executive may also have some operational management responsibilities, but as a senior leader in the organisation they have a wider remit to ensure that the organisation is fit for purpose, sustainable and ready for the future. They will need all of the competencies of a great manager, but in addition they will need to demonstrate:
- strategic and big picture thinking, a global awareness of trends, risks and opportunities and how the organisation might best meet these
- business transformation capabilities, including shaping the organisational structure, culture and behaviour
- critical thinking, analysis and decision making on complex challenges, dealing with uncertainty and ambiguity
- ability to positively influence and inspire others

- skilled in navigating internal politics, stakeholders and external relations
- commitment to and enforcement of company values, such as diversity, inclusion and sustainability.

Executive CVs should focus on achievements where they helped:
- achieve substantial organisational change
- drive business growth or opened up new opportunities
- successfully manage adverse business conditions
- change the organisation's culture for the better
- improve quality or successfully turned around something that was failing.

Executive CV example

On the following pages is an example of an executive CV for a Commercial Director that highlights the professional qualifications required for the job and the input they have made to the success of the organisation as a whole.

CV 10: Director CV

Jo Chapman

Address: Galston, AB9
Mobile: 07755 444444
Email: jc@gmail.co.uk

Career profile
Commercial Director with 20 years' experience working within the advertising business. Highly experienced in contract negotiation, preparing and winning contracts worth over £15 million in the past two years alone. Facilitated a number of strategic changes which improved the financial stability and income potential for the organisation during difficult economic conditions. Used to working in fast-paced environments, with high sensitivity to market conditions. Track record of identifying profitable growth opportunities while ensuring very careful risk management.

Career history
Commercial Director   J G Howard Group   2019–present
J G Howard is a professional services firm with turnover of £150 million and 200 staff. Major clients include blue-chip companies such as Formant & Jones, Dales Consultants and Berkshire Ltd.
- Responsible for leading a 10-person multi-disciplinary team, including finance, legal and property.
- Managed financial fall-out from the pandemic, when revenues plummeted and our cost basis needed to be reduced quickly. Created risk management plan, slimmed down the organisation's cost base and headcount, closing some regional offices and developing a recovery plan that achieved resilience in a turbulent period, in contrast to our main competitor who folded.
- Led the successful financial bid for a Dales Consultants contract worth £15 million in 2023, which has opened up a new market segment within the transport sector with substantial growth potential.
- Reviewed our procurement strategy and negotiated preferred supplier arrangements, which held cost prices during a time of rampant inflation, enabling stability on costs.
- Built a new client fee structure, which incentivised the up-take of longer-term contracts, bringing greater cash flow security during a challenging time.
- Introduced new financial management system with improved financial modelling capabilities. Finance and operational managers were upskilled in how to use this, with the improved scenario analysis enabling much more informed management decisions.
- Identified business opportunity to partner with Derwent University on a joint venture, combining their research capabilities and credibility with our market access. Led on the commercial strategy to maximise return on investment.
- Achieved cost-savings of over £2 million by using business analytics to compare cost centres and track areas of difference, which resulted in tightening of financial controls in specific areas, a more robust financial strategy and the decision to actively widen the client base to spread risk.

Commercial Lead **Wright Stationery Limited** 2014–2019

Reporting to Finance Director and responsible for three staff in this Founder-led business which was facing a number of business challenges.
- Identified business opportunity for York Design to partner with Wright Stationery to achieve cost savings of over £200,000 per annum on resource costs, premises and shared support functions.
- Project-managed the sale of sister company Celtic Document Supplies, which mitigated closure costs of more than £5 million had a sale not been agreed. All staff retained their jobs, which had been at risk.
- Improved departmental efficiency as a result of conducting work-flow assessment which highlighted log-jams. Reorganised staff roles to move to new more streamlined work processes.
- Facilitated greater liaison between Finance and front-line managers by arranging for finance staff to each spend some time in different areas of the business to increase understanding and enhance relationships. This led to managers involving Finance at an earlier stage in the budget-setting process, which subsequently improved the quality of the information being received.

Head of Management Accounts **Clarkson Toys** 2010–2014

Managing team of two for this international manufacturing company with turnover of £50 million.
- Spotted discrepancies in financial information, which uncovered fraudulent practices in a geographically remote part of the business.
- Developed new way of presenting financial information for non-financial managers that helped them to understand more easily the financial performance of their department.
- Trained and developed three new members of the Finance Department in the new financial management software.

Corporate Cost Analyst **W and H Atkins Ltd** 2008–2010
- Produced complex costing reports for senior management presentations.
- Advised department heads on financial performance against targets with recommendations where required.

Education and qualifications
- Member of ACCA since 2006, with continuous professional development on topics such as Financial and Legal Compliance, Commercial Best Practice and Bid Preparation
- Training in Leadership Development, HR Essentials for Managers, Change Management
- BSc Geography (2:i)   University of Colchestershire

CVs for internal promotions

If you are applying for an internal post, perhaps a promotion, you need to undertake at least as much, if not more, research than if you were applying for an external vacancy.

- Ask to speak to the manager, HR, or the current post-holder to find out what the job involves and to find out what the ideal candidate will offer. As an internal candidate, they are likely to give you this access and it gives you an opportunity to check your assumptions, tailor your application and show just how keen and suitable you are to the people involved in the recruitment decisions.
- Do not assume that the interview panel, even if it is your current manager, will know everything about you and your achievements, or that your good performance in your current role will be enough to convince them – it won't. You have to articulate confidently, realistically and enthusiastically why you are a great fit for the new role.
- Emphasise that you are an easy person to hire as you know the organisation, so can 'hit the ground running'. This gives you an advantage over an external hire.
- If you are in competition with another internal candidate, never criticise or try to undermine them, either subtly or overtly. Focus on the positives that you have to offer.

In Part Three, we laid the foundations for the content and structure of your CV with templates and advice for dealing with some common career challenges. It's now time to write your CV. Use Activity 10 on the following page to check you've incorporated all the elements needed.

ACTIVITY 10

YOUR CV CHECKLIST

Use the following checklist to make sure that your CV has all the right ingredients for a standout CV. ⬇ You can download this activity from **indigo.careers/standout_CVs**.

Tick when checked	✓
All factual information is accurate	☐
Contact details, including location, are included, with fully-functioning email and voicemail	☐
Career profile uses an appropriate job title, content and keywords for the roles applied for	☐
Career work experience shows relevant, achievement-related information	☐
All relevant qualifications, including training, are listed	☐
First half-page includes relevant skills and experience for target role	☐
Gives examples that show your skills and positive personal qualities	☐
Keywords are used both early on and throughout, along with positive action words	☐
Presentation of CV is impeccable, including spelling and grammar	☐
Format of CV will work with recruitment software if uploading it to site	☐
No more than two pages	☐
Ask others for feedback to check error-free and giving the right impression	☐
Use a covering email with your CV if applying for specific roles	☐

IN A NUTSHELL

This chapter has looked at some situations where CV content and layout requires slightly different treatment in order to help you present as a strong candidate. However, always remember that the same three rules will apply, regardless of your particular CV challenge:

- tailor the content to provide examples showing that you have exactly what the employer is looking for
- use a format that enables you to prove on the first page why you are the ideal candidate
- pay attention to the professional layout of the CV, which will be taken as an indication of your approach to your work.

PART FOUR

USING YOUR CV

CHAPTER 14
Building an online CV

CHAPTER 15
Sending your CV by email

CHAPTER 16
Social media profiles

CHAPTER 17
Job-search strategies

How to use your CV

Part Three showed you how to write your CV. Now you need to know what to do with it.

This section looks at other ways in which you can use this content on recruitment sites and other platforms, such as LinkedIn, as part of your personal brand.

We'll also look at the practical strategies you might use to get your CV noticed, particularly when you are looking for a new role.

14 BUILDING AN ONLINE CV

Some recruitment and employer websites will recommend building an online CV using their software, rather than uploading your own version. There are advantages and disadvantages to this.

This chapter will help you:

- understand what online CVs are and how they are used
- prepare the information you need to include in an online CV.

Building an online CV for job websites

Many commercial job sites and some employer sites will provide the option to build an online CV rather than uploading your existing CV. Some, like the NHS recruitment website TRACS, will offer *only* this option.

Online CVs are rather like the traditional application forms. There is a pre-determined format, requesting basic biographical information, career history, qualifications, etc. They also ask some pre-qualifier questions, e.g. your rights to work in the country, which need to be confirmed before you can proceed with the application. You may also have the opportunity to include a written statement to accompany an application if you are using it to apply for a particular job.

The advantage is that you know the information inputted will be in a format that is entirely compatible with the job-site database system, ensuring that your details are easily readable and searchable by employers looking for certain keywords. It's also pretty easy for you to keep a copy of frequently asked-for information in a separate Word document, which you can then copy and paste into the application with tweaks as needed depending on the job; this means you don't need to create it entirely fresh each time.

The disadvantages are that you have less control over how the information is displayed to the employer, which will most likely be more akin to a chronological CV with employment dates, etc. appearing in reverse order. You may also be asked to complete other information that you would not usually put on your CV, e.g. information about your salary or reasons for leaving jobs.

Where there is no space limit in the form's fields, list all the information you can, as the more content you provide, the better your chances for the recruitment algorithms to find you. Where there is a limit, then make sure you squeeze in relevant content in as concise a way as possible.

Table 12, opposite, has some other tips to help you increase your visibility on the database to recruiters.

TABLE 12: ADVICE ON BUILDING AN ONLINE CV	
Personal information	Make sure all contact details are correct and kept up to date.
Education	Specify educational background. Recruiters will look for particular educational qualifications, e.g. BSc Engineering, English GCSE, but you don't need to include every exam, including those you didn't do well in.
Professional qualifications	Include all professional qualifications whether they are directly relevant or not, e.g. NVQ Customer Service, CIMA membership.
Training	Include all of your training, which can include courses, coaching, self-directed learning, as well as on-the-job training – for instance, if you were shown how to use a new piece of equipment. The more content you include the better, as you are not usually constrained by space and it shows your commitment to your personal development.
Previous employers	You don't have to include every employer if you feel it doesn't do you any favours – for instance, if you only worked for them for a very short time. Instead, you could use an employer heading and describe it as 'Temporary Roles' and describe how you worked for a few employers during that time. Make sure all dates of employment with specific companies are correct, because employers will want to verify these.
Job titles	If you've an unusual job title, then use a more common job title to describe yourself so you are more likely to appear in keyword searches used by the recruiters to find candidates on the database.
Experience	An outline of your main duties and responsibilities is usually required under each role you have worked in. Don't just summarise your job description. Instead, emphasise activities that are relevant to your target role, along with some achievements that show you are a high performer.
Skills	Include as many skills as you can justify, including any different terms to describe them. This is an important field that recruiters use to find candidates with the skills they require.
Location	These forms will often ask your location and/or your preference for working remotely. Complete both so that you are included in searches for all opportunities; you can then decide which ones are right for you.
Salary	The form usually asks you for your salary requirements or your last salary. It enables the recruiter to assess your seniority level in your field. Wherever possible, indicate a salary range to give you some room for manoeuvre. Look for a salary survey on the internet to get an idea of the market value if you are unsure.

Sector	Recruiters often look for specific sector experience in their candidate searches. Tick each sector you have worked in, even if they were short-term roles.
Keywords	Using the information from Activity 8, sprinkle your keywords throughout your online CV. Sometimes there is also a section for 'additional information' where you can input these.
Covering letter	If you are applying for a specific job, some sites provide the option to write a covering letter to accompany your CV. Always take this opportunity. While it won't in itself influence the shortlisting algorithm, it will work in your favour when the recruiter reads it alongside your CV, because few other candidates will have bothered and this will show your conscientiousness. See Chapter 15 for advice on covering letters.

Job notifications

To save time on searching for roles, you can set up automatic notifications for jobs that meet the criteria you are interested in.

Many of the sites use what is called 'semantic search', which can also send you details of roles that you may not have specified, but which the algorithms have interpreted rightly or wrongly as having similarities. To avoid getting inundated by roles you are not interested in, you can further narrow your search by using 'AND', 'OR' and 'AND NOT' to make your keyword search as specific as you need; you can also use quote marks to group terms. For example, if you want to be a Marketing Manager but don't want PR to be part of your role, you should type 'Marketing Manager' AND NOT 'PR Manager'.

IN A NUTSHELL

- An online CV will display your information in an appropriate and easily keyword-searchable form.
- You can copy and paste content from your CV into the fields in the online form.
- Always remember to include your keywords.
- Write a covering letter where the option is provided.
- Set up automatic notifications for job listings, but be selective in the criteria you use or you are likely to be inundated.

15 SENDING YOUR CV BY EMAIL

You have spent considerable time and effort in researching and writing your CV. However, even with a great CV you can inadvertently sabotage your chances if you don't pay sufficient attention to the way in which you send your CV to the employer.

This chapter will help you:

- ensure your CV lands well when it is emailed
- write a covering email to accompany your attached CV.

The growth in technology has meant that most recruitment is now largely conducted via a digital platform, through which the employer will seek to find and shortlist candidates.

However, there are still occasions when you may be required to send your CV directly to an individual or a department, in which case there are some additional things that are useful to know.

Format compatibility

It's possible, even if you are sending your CV via email, that the recipient may still upload your CV onto their in-house recruitment system, so the same rules apply in ensuring that your CV is likely to be readable by their database, i.e. standard fonts, layouts and margins.

If you know for certain that your CV will not be uploaded into an in-house system, then send your CV in PDF format; this gives you the option to use different creative designs for your CV.

Email etiquette

- Always write a covering email to accompany any CV you are sending directly to an individual or a company, including agencies or headhunters. It gives you the chance to give context to your application, explain your enthusiasm and show a little of your personality.
- Make sure you use and spell people's names correctly, otherwise you are irritating them from the start. In your covering email, write in full sentences, but use bullet points to emphasise relevant experience and skills .
- Never use text-speak as you would on your mobile; end the message formally, e.g. 'I look forward to hearing from you', rather than 'Thx!'.
- Always check and double-check the spelling in the main body of your email and any attachments.
- When sending your CV as an attachment, always label the attachment with your full name to make it easy for them to find it once they have downloaded it. If you are applying for a particular job, then include this in the document

name too, e.g. msmith604execpa.doc. These measures ensure that your CV will be easily identified, especially if you have a common name.
- Don't use your work email address to send job applications, set up a private email account instead.
- Exercise caution in sending out your personal details. Is this a company that you know or which you can verify independently? If you are unsure, take a look on the web and see if you can find out anything about the company before sending out your confidential information. Identity fraud is sadly commonplace now, and the information on your CV, your contact details, occupation, etc. could be of high value to someone who wanted to pretend to be someone else.

Writing a covering email for your CV

If your CV is attached to the email, then use the main body of the email as your covering letter. This is an opportunity to make a great first impression as to why you are a great candidate and persuade them to open the attachment and look at your CV in more detail. See the example below.

EMAIL COVERING LETTER

To: Ann Brown
Subject: Executive Personal Assistant role, Ref No. 1234
Attachment: MWoodExecAsstfeb23.doc

Dear Ann

I am writing to express my keen interest in the Executive Personal Assistant position at ETD. I believe that my background and experience make me a strong candidate for this role, as I offer the following:

- Over 10 years of experience as an Executive Assistant, supporting Directors and CEOs in high-pressure roles

- Highly efficient and versatile multi-tasker, capable of diary scheduling, managing events, report writing, problem-solving, liaising with staff and stakeholders, and welcoming VIPs, often all at the same time

- Proactive approach, priding myself on my ability to anticipate Directors' needs, whether it is preparing briefing papers, avoiding diary clashes or escalating critical issues for attention

- Excellent interpersonal skills, including diplomacy and confidentiality, which are so essential when entrusted to deal with matters of great sensitivity
- Excellent IT skills, including advanced knowledge of Microsoft Office Suite, calendar management tools and database systems. Additionally, I am experienced in training others in these tools.

I understand that ETD currently has ambitious plans for developing its international market, and I believe that my experience working for global firms will be an advantage.

My attached CV offers further details on my experience, and I hope to meet you to discuss this opportunity further.

Best wishes

Maria Wood
07777 555555

Using AI

You can also use AI to help you construct your covering email. Here are some suggested AI prompts.

AI prompt	How to use the prompt and the AI response
Find me the latest news about... (insert company)? *What are the business challenges faced by...* (insert company name) *and similar ones in...* (insert field or sector)?	Refer to this research in your covering email to show that you have done your homework and are thoughtful about what this company needs, e.g. 'My background in compliance will be an asset to your company, given the new incoming regulations around...'
Help me write a covering email for a job application as a... (insert job title).	You can ask it to produce a few versions, perhaps focused on skills, achievements or emphasising the personality fit. Mix and match from the versions it produces, adding in your own content to personalise it.
Copy your CV into the AI prompt and ask it: *Use this content to create a covering email for a job as...* (insert job title).	It will produce a version of a covering email that you can edit.
Make more concise. *Summarise this in 200 words.*	If the covering email version that the AI produces is too long, either use this prompt or give it a target word count.

Here's an example of how AI helped with ideas for a covering email for a role as Project Manager in the Hotel Industry.

Ask AI: *What are the challenges faced by the hotel industry?*

AI answer: *The hotel industry faces several business challenges, including:*
- *Labor Shortages: Difficulty in finding and retaining skilled and reliable staff.*
- *Seasonal Demand Fluctuations: Managing resources efficiently to handle peak and off-peak periods.*
- *Intense Competition: Competing with other hotels and alternative accommodations.*
- *Changing Customer Expectations: Adapting to evolving guest preferences and demands.*
- *Online Travel Agencies (OTAs): High commissions impacting profitability.*
- *Regulatory Compliance: Navigating various industry regulations and standards.*
- *Online Reputation Management: Dealing with online reviews and maintaining a positive image.*
- *Cybersecurity and Data Privacy: Protecting customer data from cyber threats.*
- *Rising Operating Costs: Managing expenses related to utilities, supplies, and maintenance.*
- *Economic Fluctuations: Sensitivity to economic cycles affecting travel and spending.*
- *Impact of Natural Disasters and Health Crises: Dealing with disruptions caused by unforeseen events.*
- *Sustainability Concerns: Implementing eco-friendly practices and initiatives.*
- *Keeping up with Technology: Adopting and integrating new technologies to enhance operations and guest experiences.*
- *Global Political Uncertainty: Turbulence and geopolitical events affecting international travel.*

To succeed, hotels must prioritize customer satisfaction, efficiency, and strategic planning while staying responsive to industry trends.

Ask AI: *Using this information, write me a covering email for a job as a Project Manager in the hotel industry.*

AI answer: *[see below]*

AI COVERING LETTER

Dear Hiring Manager,

I am writing to express my keen interest in the position of Project Manager at [Hotel Name]. With a strong background in project management and a deep understanding of the challenges faced by the hotel industry, I am confident that I can contribute significantly to the success of your esteemed organization.

Throughout my career, I have successfully led and executed diverse projects, including renovations, technology implementations, and process improvements, in the hospitality sector. The challenges presented by labor shortages, seasonal demand fluctuations, and ever-changing customer expectations have honed my ability to adapt swiftly and strategically to deliver exceptional results.

One of the key strengths I possess is my expertise in fostering collaboration and communication among cross-functional teams. I firmly believe that effective teamwork is vital for overcoming intense competition and accomplishing project objectives with precision and efficiency. My experience in liaising with various stakeholders, including hotel staff, suppliers, and management, has consistently led to seamless project execution and enhanced guest experiences.

Moreover, my passion for technology integration and commitment to cybersecurity and data privacy align well with the hotel industry's growing reliance on innovative solutions and guest data protection. I am adept at evaluating and implementing cutting-edge technologies to optimize operations and elevate service standards.

As a Project Manager, I understand the significance of maintaining regulatory compliance and ensuring sustainable practices within the hotel environment. I have a proven track record of spearheading sustainability initiatives that not only positively impact the environment but also contribute to cost-saving measures.

Having navigated through challenging times such as natural disasters and health crises, I am well-prepared to proactively address unforeseen disruptions and drive your hotel's resilience.

I am genuinely excited about the opportunity to contribute my expertise and enthusiasm to [Hotel Name]'s continued success.

Thank you for considering my application. Please find my resumé attached for your reference.

Sincerely

The AI response helpfully highlights some of the key business issues in the sector and how the candidate can help address these as a Project Manager. The above version is too long, uses Americanisms and feels somewhat superficial, but it does give a useful structure and some very helpful ideas that you can adapt for your own covering email. Remember, you can't just use the AI version itself – it has to be authentic to you, edited and personalised, with concrete examples of your achievements and skills, otherwise it will look like everyone else's who has also used AI. As we highlighted right at the start of this book, it is a criminal offence to lie on your CV, so don't misrepresent yourself. You know who you are better than the AI does.

TABLE 13: CHECKLIST FOR EMAILING CVs	
Tick when checked	✓
Your CV attachment if sending in Microsoft Word:	
• Standard font, e.g. Calibri or Times New Roman, size 10–12 for body of text and size 14 for headings	☐
• Standard margin lengths	☐
• Bold used sparingly, principally for headings	☐
• No columns or boxes	☐
• No graphics, photos or Jpegs	☐
• No shading	☐
CV attachment if sending as PDF:	
• Checked that recipient/website can upload or view these	☐
CV attachment sending from or to a Mac:	
• Double-check format to ensure CV is compatible with recipient's software	☐
Has all the spelling and grammar in the email covering letter been double-checked?	☐
Have you specified in the Subject Line of email the vacancy/reference number of the job for which you are applying?	☐
Does the email covering letter state why you are a good candidate?	☐
Is the covering letter written formally, using full sentences with bullet points to reinforce key selling points?	☐
Have you addressed the individual by name, if known, in the covering letter?	☐
Have you labelled your CV attachment with your name?	☐
Have you created an email address just for job-searching?	☐
Have you included your telephone number in the main body of your email to make it easy for people to contact you?	☐

IN A NUTSHELL

This chapter has helped ensure that when you send your CV by email, you continue to reinforce the image of you as a highly professional and capable candidate. Remember that:

- all communication with an employer is formal and needs great care and attention to show your professionalism
- AI can provide ideas and a useful structure for your covering emails, but you have to ensure that the version you send is authentic.

16 SOCIAL MEDIA PROFILES

These present excellent opportunities for marketing yourself to potential employers and for advertising your professional brand, i.e. who you are, what you do and how you do it.

This chapter will help you:

- understand what social media is
- know how to use different social media to your advantage
- manage your web presence and your online reputation.

What is social media?

Social media refers to online platforms that enable users to discover and interact with each other, sharing information, opinions, photos and videos. While some started out as being primarily for professional or personal use, the boundaries have become increasingly blurry and need careful management.

LinkedIn

Your CV is normally only seen either by those to whom you have sent it directly, or by recruiters who have paid for access to the candidate database of a recruitment website. By contrast, LinkedIn is a website that enables your online CV and business profile to be seen directly by the wider world. It puts your CV into the public domain. You can choose to restrict the information about you that is available publicly, but this rather defeats the object of being on there in the first place if you are looking for your next role.

While some people may feel uncomfortable about sharing their CV information in this way, if you are *not* one of the 930 million users on the site, then you are missing out on a great opportunity to advertise yourself to prospective employers and be approached by recruiters and headhunters.

You can use the CV you have created using this book within your LinkedIn profile, copying large sections across as required. However, there are some important differences, so let's look at the ingredients that are essential to creating an attractive and persuasive CV profile on LinkedIn.

- **Photo.** Unlike your CV, it is recommended you do include a photo on your LinkedIn profile. According to LinkedIn, members with a profile photo have 21 times more views and up to nine times more connection requests than members who don't. You can also include a short introductory video that activates if someone clicks on your photo.
- **Headline title.** This is rather like the strapline for a company – it explains what you do. You have up to 150 words to explain who you are professionally and the value you bring to an organisation. It needs to be clear, concise and positive in tone. Crucially, it also needs to include the industry keywords that

are expressive of your role, so that people searching for someone with your skills can find you. For instance:

- Award-winning Graphic Designer | Transforming brands with wit and imagination
- Data Analyst | Advanced Excel | Predictive Analytics | SQL | Helping business make informed decisions
- Executive PA | Superb administrative support | Making your life easier | Born organiser
- HR Manager | Driving organisational performance and developing a future-fit workforce
- Digital Marketing Strategist | Helping brands maximise online visibility and engagement
- Leadership Development Coach | Empowering professionals to unlock their full potential
- Project Manager | Agile Methodologies | Cross-functional Team Leadership | PMP Certified
- Software Engineer | Full Stack Development | Python | JavaScript | Agile methodologies

ASK AI

Copy your CV or your CV profile into the AI chat and ask it to produce 10 suggestions for a LinkedIn profile based on this content using no more than 150 words.
OR
Ask AI for suggestions for a LinkedIn Headline suitable for your line of work. For instance, I asked AI to give me five suggestions for a headline for a Business Development Manager. These were the results:

- *Business Development Manager | Driving revenue growth through strategic partnerships and market expansion*
- *Results-Driven Business Development Manager | Cultivating profitable client relationships and identifying new market opportunities*
- *Business Development Manager | Creating winning strategies for sales growth and market penetration*
- *Experienced Business Development Manager | Developing high-value accounts and negotiating complex deals*
- *Business Development Manager | Driving market share expansion and maximizing revenue generation*

- **About You section.** This is similar to the summary profile on your CV, although you have more room to describe yourself, provide some context and let readers know what you are interested in. As with your regular CV, readers are only going to superficially scan your profile, so make sure that all of the impressive stuff is up top, especially your achievements, and if you can name-drop, here is the place to do it. Again, make sure that there are lots of the keywords in your field mentioned in this profile to aid your searchability.
- **Employment history.** As in your CV, your LinkedIn profile gives you the option to include details of your experience. Ensure it is achievement-focused, showing how you have added value to your organisation, rather than just providing a list of factual information about dates and duties. You can be a little bit more circumspect about quantifying data on this profile as it is public, and you don't necessarily want to be sharing commercial secrets.
- **Skills.** List your top skills. This is a key section used by search software to find candidates. According to LinkedIn, those who have five or more skills listed are contacted 27 times more by employers than others.
- **Endorsements.** Companies often use positive feedback from customers to persuade other potential buyers. LinkedIn takes this idea and allows you to include personal testimonials. Ask people you know, whether it is your manager, colleagues, customers, suppliers or friends to write a few positive words about your work capabilities on your LinkedIn page. You can send them a testimonial request through LinkedIn, and also make suggestions for the kind of thing you would like them to write to keep them on-message with the image you are trying to portray. The fact that another individual has taken the time to write positive things for and about you will be viewed by others as an indication of credibility and authenticity.
- **Supporting information.** Your LinkedIn profile can include other materials that you feel will help you stand out from other candidates, such as videos, presentations, links to websites or media features. If you are a creative professional, such as a graphic designer, and want the viewer of your LinkedIn page to see examples of your work, you can also append a creative portfolio display, although there are limitations on size.
- **Connections.** LinkedIn is a fantastic tool to help you build a structured business networking grapevine. You can search for anyone that you know, either in a work or personal context, and link up with them electronically so

that you can swap information, ideas and updates. If you are interested in a particular company, then you can also search through LinkedIn to see if anyone you know works there and send them a message.
- **Activity updates.** Rather like X (formerly Twitter), you can send short messages from your LinkedIn page to all of your LinkedIn connections. You can use this as part of your own personal PR campaign to remind people about you and what you can offer, or share news about any business successes, events or feedback from a happy customer. You can also send out comments or questions on current topics to encourage a dialogue with people in your network.
- **LinkedIn groups.** There are groups on the site for every professional niche. Some of these groups are open to anyone who shows an interest, while others have exclusive criteria. Join groups that are relevant to you. Introduce yourself to the other members of the group, and participate in discussions where you feel you can add a useful perspective and/or want to engage with particular users. Recruiters, employers and managers will also be members of this group, and if there is someone that seems to be of interest, then they may well click onto your full LinkedIn profile to find out more.
- **Advertised jobs.** LinkedIn will automatically send you jobs that the algorithm thinks you may be interested in based on your headline and job titles. If you are being sent roles that are unsuitable, then this is a good sign that you need to amend your content.
- **Opentowork.** LinkedIn suggests you use this marker on your profile if you are actively seeking new opportunities. It's a useful way to let your connections know that you are looking, and for recruiters to know you are available. However, unlike job websites, the attraction of LinkedIn is that recruiters can approach anyone, whether they are actively looking for a job or not, so it may make little difference.
- **Premium services.** Basic membership of LinkedIn is free, but you can upgrade your account if you wish to access additional features, such as enhanced search and the 'in-mail' function. The upgrades are especially suitable for those who are themselves recruiters or who are using LinkedIn for business development purposes.

LinkedIn warning

Your LinkedIn profile is public, which means that anyone can look at it, including your current employer, colleagues, business contacts, peers, as well as prospective employers. This means any discrepancies between your CV and people's experiences of working with you are going to be very obvious. Make sure the content is factually accurate, including your employment dates, qualifications and achievements.

The LinkedIn site has lots of advice and guidance about how to get started on LinkedIn, and updates on new features. See **www.LinkedIn.com** for more information.

YouTube

Creating video content and uploading it to YouTube or another video hosting site, like Vimeo, can be a very effective way to showcase your professional expertise, whether you are a subject expert, a trainer, a presenter or you want to display examples of your work — for instance, footage of gardens you have designed, media clips or events you have organised. These clips can then also be added to the multimedia section of your LinkedIn profile, your website or other social media profiles.

Video CVs that feature you talking through your CV or giving your 'sales pitch' on why you are a good person to hire, are not recommended unless this is something that the company has expressly asked for. Videos are very tricky to get right, both in terms of their look and feel. It may be free to upload your video to YouTube and cheap to send a video file via email, but a poor quality video can do your prospects more harm than good.

Blogs, podcasts, webinars

If you want to raise your profile as an expert or influencer in your field, then writing articles or creating podcasts or webinars are good ways to raise visibility in your field. However, it's very time-intensive to create this content, and you are competing for attention in a very crowded market; you need to either have access to a ready-made audience channel or be very marketing savvy to engage the attention of new audiences.

Your digital reputation

Employers have become extremely sensitive to the digital footprint of employees and candidates applying to their organisation.

It is very easy for HR professionals or managers to research potential candidates on the internet. Some recruiters do this search as a matter of course. They may or may not tell you that they are doing so, but if they find any comments or behaviour that they don't like or are unsure about, you are unlikely to hear from them.

So, a word of warning! Be very careful about everything you share online, even if you think the privacy settings protect you, because they don't always.

> *The implications of social networking sites for recruitment are quite significant. Look at your social pages from an outsider's point of view. If there are pictures of you falling out of a nightclub door, what image does this give to a potential employer? Keep your public profile brief, but professional. Be wary of putting anything negative in the public domain that could affect your reputation.*
>
> Adrian Marsh, Career Coach

IN A NUTSHELL

- Use social networking sites, such as LinkedIn, to extend the reach of your CV to prospective employers.
- Consider adding multimedia content, like videos, articles and endorsements, as part of your CV portfolio which you can share on LinkedIn and other social media sites.
- Build connections online to raise your visibility in your field.
- Make sure your website presence remains professional at all times.

17 JOB-SEARCH STRATEGIES

You are now ready to use your CV. So where is your ideal job? This chapter provides advice on how to find it.

This chapter will help you:

- tackle the advertised job market

- uncover hidden jobs through networking and speculative approaches

- understand what recruitment agencies and headhunters want from your CV.

Let's look at the main job search strategies in turn, and how you can use your CV to good effect.

Advertised jobs

Job websites are usually the first place people look for a new job. There are sites that cover a range of jobs, like **www.indeed.com**, **www.CV-library.co.uk** and government websites like **www.gov.uk/find-a-job**. There are also websites specialising in certain professional fields, such as **https://jobs.accaglobal.com** for accountancy and finance roles, or **www.eteach.co.uk** for education professionals.

LinkedIn is also used by many recruiters to advertise jobs, and will even suggest roles to you based on your job title and skills, even if you are not actively looking for a job. Additionally, most large employers have a careers page on their own website where you can apply directly for vacancies.

The advantage of using these websites is that they are very convenient. You can upload your details and a CV onto the site so that you are visible to recruiters searching for candidates. You can set up email alerts so that you are notified every time a suitable new role is advertised, and then you can apply for the jobs with only a couple of mouse clicks.

The disadvantage is that the high visibility of these adverts and the convenience factor means that there is a lot of competition for roles, and you will be scored by recruitment software algorithms. Your score will depend on how well your CV matches the recruiters' search terms in respect of your job title, skills and experience, qualifications, seniority, sector, salary expectations and location. You can be a highly suitable candidate, but if your CV doesn't work with the software algorithms, or if you receive a similar high score to others but they are just listed higher than you, then recruiters may already have made a decision about whom to invite to interview before they even read your CV.

Faking it?

Thousands of jobs are advertised on job website boards, but it is sometimes difficult to validate how genuine and current some of those jobs are. Where jobs are posted by an employer, you can usually check whether the job is genuine by checking if it is also posted on their corporate website. However, many of the jobs posted on internet recruitment boards are from agencies, so it is doubly difficult to check.

Unfortunately, there is anecdotal evidence to suggest that there are agencies out there that advertise non-existent jobs simply to boost their candidate database. A typical scenario is that a great sounding job is advertised with excellent pay and conditions but few specific criteria. This guarantees a large response from a wide pool. Candidates who apply then never hear anything or are told almost immediately that the vacancy has been filled but their details will be kept on file, even though the advertisement may continue to be posted or reappear at some later date.

Why do some agencies do this? Many vacancies are filled via a first past the post situation, so the quicker the agency can get a suitable candidate in front of an employer the more chance they have of getting their commission. These agencies need a ready stock of good quality, available clients. If their stocks are running low, then advertising a 'dream job' is an ideal way to pull in good-quality candidates, even if it is against the Recruitment and Employment Confederation's Code of Practice.

Publicity shy?

It is important to consider how public you want your CV to be on these job-search websites. Of course, you want all recruiters to be able to see your CV, but you may not want your colleagues, competitors or even your boss to see it.

Some sites offer a facility whereby you can block access to your CV from particular organisations. Alternatively, you can grant access to the main body of your CV, but remove your personal data and contact information. However, bear in mind that you may still be identifiable from your list of employers, educational details, etc.

Making your CV completely confidential means that you can still look for jobs and forward your CV for opportunities that look interesting, but you will miss out on the recruiters browsing through the database looking for suitable candidates. There is a difficult balance to be sought between advertising your skills and retaining privacy and security.

Anyone can pay a fee to a commercial job website company to post positions on the site and/or search through the CVs in the database. The vast majority of people who want to do this are, of course, employers and recruitment agencies. However, you only need to see the amount of pop-ups and advertisements on many of the job sites to see that job-seekers are also a target audience for many other companies seeking to market their services.

Most troubling is that there have been instances where job-seekers posting their CVs on websites and social networking sites have been the target of criminal activity. Fake jobs have been used as a means to extract money from candidates and obtain national insurance (NI) numbers, even bank details – it's a goldmine for anyone wanting to commit identity theft.

Be assured that you should never have to pay anyone to find you work; this is a fundamental principle of the UK Employment Agencies Act. The only exceptions are in the entertainment and modelling sectors, where agents represent the 'talent'.

It's always useful to check the credentials of any company you are dealing with when they are strangers to you, and if something feels odd then check it out with someone else you trust, because your gut instinct is often right.

All of the above means that, while you should definitely be looking at advertised jobs on recruitment, social media and other websites, there are other job search strategies you should also be using.

Networking

You may have heard people talk about the advertised and unadvertised job market. Statistics vary, but it is estimated that perhaps 80% of jobs are never advertised or, if they are, the successful candidate has heard about the role in a way other than reading the advertisement. Interestingly, these statistics apply regardless of the type of role sought, so it is as relevant whether you are a first time job-seeker or a CEO.

Other people are a major source of information about prospective jobs and employers. No-one will give you a job just because they know you, but they will tell you about potential opportunities or people you could contact. Be clear about the kind of role/organisation you are looking for and ask **anyone and everyone** you know if they have got any advice for you or ideas on whom you should contact. **This is a highly successful method of job search!** Remember to keep your contacts updated on your progress and feed back to them if they have put you in touch with someone they know.

WHO KNOWS WHOM

The leading social scientist Professor Mark Granovetter conducted extensive research on networking, and found that individuals who were more socially connected were generally much more successful when looking for a new job. He also found that it was often their indirect acquaintances – or those he called 'weak ties' – who were most helpful to people in their careers. Widening your circle, asking your contacts if they know of anyone else who could help you, is proven to be a very effective career management strategy.

In a workplace where hybrid working has reduced the professional social connections most people have ready to hand, it's become even more important that you actively cultivate connections both within work and externally. This isn't about racking up the numbers of connections you have on LinkedIn. This is about building genuine dialogue, ideally in person but perhaps virtually too. Talk to people in your own organisation (perhaps in different departments), attend industry meet-ups, catch up with ex-colleagues or join a professional association. Extending your contacts means that they or someone they know could be very helpful to you in the future.

Speculative approaches

If you are interested in working for a particular company, try to find someone who works there whom you can talk to. They might be able to arrange an introduction, give advice on the best way to apply or the manager you should write to.

You'll need to prepare a carefully crafted email outlining your experience and what you offer that will be useful to them. You don't necessarily need to send your CV at this point, the aim is more to generate interest and start a conversation. You can send a CV once you are clearer about what you think they have an appetite for.

This proactive approach can be highly successful if you send your CV to a named individual within a company who is in a position to hire you, i.e. the relevant manager. They will know what their immediate and anticipated recruitment needs are and precisely the skills they will be looking for. Don't send it to the Human Resources (HR) department, as they are likely to refer you to their vacancies page.

The advantage of this speculative type of approach is that there are often no other candidates in competition with you, and you represent a cheap way for the organisation to recruit, i.e. no agency or advertising costs. Its success depends on the strength of your research, the marketing of your skills — and timing. Your email may just land in the inbox at the right time. Opposite is a sample speculative email.

As with the covering emails we discussed in Chapter 15, you can also use AI to help you research companies and provide a useful structure for your speculative email.

> **SPECULATIVE EMAIL**
>
> To: Raj Patel
> Subject: Opportunity to work together
>
> Dear Raj
>
> I hope this email finds you well.
>
> Gina Roberts recommended I get in touch, as she thought my extensive experience in Brand Management within the luxury automotive industry might be of particular interest to Gladstone Inc.
>
> I've been privileged to work with renowned brands, such as Ferrari, Porsche and Lexus, with some of my proudest achievements including:
>
> - 20% increase in merchandising sales for Ferrari through developing new product lines and licensing arrangements in emerging markets
> - project-managing a global marketing campaign for Porsche, which cleverly leveraged local market insights, driving a 10% increase in sales leads
> - organising large-scale corporate events at Formula 1, high-profile charity balls and celebrity galas maximising brand exposure and prestige
> - 30% increase in online engagement for the Lexus brand by utilising lifestyle channels and influencers to expand customer reach.
>
> I'm currently looking at new opportunities, so would be very interested to talk with you to explore possibilities on either a permanent or a project basis.
>
> Kind regards
>
> Simon McAllister
> Mobile: 07555 555 555

Recruitment agencies

Employers pay recruitment agencies to find suitable candidates. An agency may be the sole agency working with the employer, or it may be in competition with other agencies. Usually, only the agency whose candidate is selected will receive the commission from the employer.

Recruitment agencies are therefore often under considerable time pressure. This means that they are interested in having clients whom they can easily place. Your CV needs to be very focused and clear about what you want and why you are suitable. If you are looking for a career change, you may find a recruitment agent less helpful. In a highly competitive market, agencies will understandably prioritise obvious candidates over those who it may take a little more imagination to see in the role. It is worth remembering that agencies are under no obligation to put you forward for any roles. They are not working for you, but for the employer.

Sometimes agencies will want you to reformat your CV in their own house style. This is fine. However, they should discuss with you if they plan to make any edits to the content. They usually take off your contact details to ensure that employers can't hire you directly and cut them out of their commission.

Agencies have a recruitment database system where they will store your CV and the information it contains. They will use keyword searches to research the database for candidates who match the requirements of a particular job. They are also likely to trawl LinkedIn to look for individuals who may not be actively looking but who could be a good fit.

When applying for a job through an agency, there is often less opportunity to tailor your CV to a particular employer's requirements, because they want to move quickly and don't always tell you the employer's details until the last minute. However, if you are invited to interview, ask for the job description and person specification and use this to update your CV to their requirements, and send them the new version ahead of the interview.

Headhunters

Headhunters tend to be executive agencies that are tasked by an employer to find senior level candidates. They will use their existing database of candidates, act on recommendations from people in the industry, and use LinkedIn to identify individuals of interest.

> *Headhunters are impressed by clarity and conciseness. A CV should be neither too long nor too short. It must communicate as much as possible but must never tire or bore the reader. The CV must show the organisations for whom the individual worked what they do or did, the size of the organisation, the scale of the role(s) held. More detail should be given to more recent employment. Include key financial metrics such as turnover, profitability (if possible), headcount and budgets. Achievements should be within the section on the relevant employer rather than positioned in a separate section. Anonymity of employment should be avoided at all costs as should generalities on personal characteristics.*
>
> Áine Hurley, Odgers Berndtson

Headhunters tend to operate in niche areas, so look on the internet for those who operate within your field and send them your CV with a covering email so that you are on their radar.

Cultivate relationships with headhunters, as they can be important door-openers for you; even if they don't have an opportunity for you right now, they can provide a valuable insight into the job market, what is in demand and how you benchmark.

You can increase the likelihood of your being headhunted by:

- having a professional profile on LinkedIn
- being visible in your industry by being involved in public events, working groups, your professional institute, appearing in webinars
- positioning yourself as an industry influencer, sharing insights, speaking at conferences, presenting research or thought leadership
- being a good networker, and well connected with a positive reputation.

IN A NUTSHELL

- Follow application instructions exactly as requested for advertised jobs.
- Always include a covering email with your CV.
- Send a one-page CV for speculative approaches.
- Make sure you personalise each speculative approach.
- Agencies want candidates who are easy to place. Be clear about what you want and give them a CV that presents you as an obvious candidate for that kind of role.
- Increase your visibility if you want to be headhunted.

ADDITIONAL RESOURCES

PART FIVE

CHAPTER 18
Other resources

CHAPTER 19
And finally…

18 OTHER RESOURCES

This chapter outlines some additional external resources that you may find helpful, either in the CV writing process or in meeting your larger job-search or career-management objectives.

This chapter will help you:

- identify the range of free resources that can assist you in devising your CV

- examine some of the commercial career support services available and suggest selection criteria.

Other people

One of the most challenging aspects of writing a CV is to remain objective about yourself. It can be easy to underplay your skills or 'over-egg' your achievements. So one of the most valuable resources you can utilise is other people.

Try to get a second opinion on your CV from one or more people who know you, whose opinion you trust and who are willing and able to give you honest feedback. Ideally, they will know you in a work context and have some knowledge about recruitment and/or your target role. Brief them on the job you are looking for, and then ask for their opinion on:

- whether the content makes sense and is relevant
- whether the CV looks good (attractive layout, spelling, etc.)
- what impression they think your CV creates and whether it matches the one you were aiming for.

Very often they will be able to flag up areas on your CV that are unclear, or where too much or too little detail is provided. You may get some different, even conflicting views, but most importantly you will get some consistent messages regarding what works and what doesn't. This will help you develop a CV that is robust enough to work for all the different recruiters to whom your CV is going to be sent.

Free career support services

In the UK, there are a number of different resources where you can access careers and job-search information for free.

- The National Careers Service provides careers information and guidance via its website (**https://nationalcareersservice.direct.gov.uk**).
- Students can usually access a free in-house careers service at their university or college.
- There may be other career support initiatives for particular communities, such as apprenticeships, women-returners, or those facing barriers to

finding employment. These may be funded by governmental sources or by voluntary organisations. You can often hear about these through your local Job Centre or community groups.
- Many career-related websites offer free job-searching information and tips on CV writing; you can find useful articles on many topics on **www.personalcareermanagement.com** and **LinkedIn**.
- If you are looking to work in a particular sector, it is well worth checking out the website of the relevant professional body or institutions. They frequently offer information on recruitment in their field.
- There are also sector- or organisation-specific websites that can help, e.g. **www.nhscareers.nhs.uk**, which provides advice and help for anyone interested in working with the NHS, whether they are looking for a clinical or non-clinical role.

Commercial services

Many of the 'free services' listed above can be extremely helpful. However, because they cater for huge audiences, the advice tends to be generic, and the opportunities for meaningful discussions about your particular career situation are limited.

Commercial services, on the whole, will offer you more individual and customised support, although this too can vary. Listed below are some of the more popular paid-for career services.

CV writing services

There are CV companies on the internet which offer a free CV review: assessing your CV in terms of its content, format and keyword visibility to rate how well it is likely to fare with the recruitment software of an online Applicant Tracking System. It can be useful to get this feedback; however, these companies usually want you to upgrade to their paid-for CV services, so this feedback may not be completely objective.

Prices for CV writing services can range from as little as £50 to over £1,000, but the quality and service is variable and not always commensurate with the price.

How it typically works is that you will send a copy of your current CV and/or complete a questionnaire. There may also be a conversation with the person who will be writing your CV. The finished CV is then emailed to you.

The advantages of using this type of service is that the CV is usually attractively presented and they are produced pretty quickly, often within a week. The disadvantage is that the limited amount of discussion the individual has with the CV writer means that there is often a formulaic approach to writing the CV, with an over-reliance on stock phrases. You can end up with a CV that doesn't sound like you at all, and which may appear insincere and insubstantial.

In addition, if you are at all unsure or unfocused about your next role, then this hesitancy is likely to show up in your CV, regardless of who wrote it. If you are thinking of making a career change, then your CV is likely to require a lot more thought and discussion than a CV writing service may be able to offer and deliver.

When considering this service, it is perhaps most important to be realistic in your expectations to avoid disappointment. While there is no guarantee that the more expensive CV writing services are better than the cheapest, it is unrealistic to expect a CV for which you have paid less than £100 to have hours of input lavished on it. You can reasonably expect some prettying up of the presentation, but not a lot else. Some companies will be honest with you about this, others more vague.

If you are considering a CV writing service, here are some guidelines to help you choose.

- Choose companies whose websites are well written, clear, functional and aesthetically pleasing. A poorly presented website does not give confidence that your CV will be as professionally produced as required. (NB: There are CV writing websites with prominent spelling mistakes on their home page!)
- Be clear on the brief you are giving your CV writer. Highlight the key points you want to emphasise and provide the detail they require.
- Aim for companies that include consultation time between you and the CV writer.
- Try to find out how much time is allocated for the CV writer to spend on

physically writing your CV so you can gauge what degree of input and thought is likely to go into its production.
- Check out the credentials of the person writing your CV and what qualifies them to do this work.
- Ensure you are clear on all costs and what is included for the price.
- Confirm the response time so everyone is clear about the timescale expectation.

AI CV services

Many new commercial CV writing services have emerged using AI. As we have seen, AI can be extremely helpful in providing a structure and suggestions for the type of content to include on your CV for particular types of jobs. It's also very good at writing the content in a clear, fluent and grammatically accurate way.

However, despite its seeming promise, you can't just delegate your CV writing to AI. It needs thought, personalisation and authenticity. Otherwise, your CV will be dismissed as superficial and be indistinguishable from the millions of other users asking AI to write their CV for them.

Career coach

A career coach is typically someone who will work with you on a one-to-one basis to help support you in creating the working life you want. This may be in the form of face-to-face meetings or virtual video coaching. The coaching element means that this service is more personal, and therefore better able to consider your whole career story and needs.

There are career-management companies, like Personal Career Management (**www.personalcareermanagement.com**), which specialise in working with individuals to help them make informed career decisions and support them in finding their next role. This can be particularly helpful if you are feeling stuck in your career, want to explore your options and would benefit from support in the job-search process, including devising your CV, help with interview skills, etc.

There are also outplacement companies which focus primarily on providing job-searching support to individuals who have been made redundant. Many of these will work with individuals only if their organisation is paying for their support. However, there are some who will work with private individuals who are funding themselves.

You may also be able to find a freelance career coach who will offer career-related coaching options according to their particular expertise.

The advantage of using a career coach is that they can advise you on the more practical aspects of job-searching while working with you on some of the more personal aspects, like presenting a confident image, achieving a work/life balance or working out what you really want to do. The CV is only one aspect of managing your career and making the career change you want. Career coaches are particularly helpful if you are experiencing a career block and are uncertain or unfocused on what to do next.

The disadvantage is that they usually require a larger financial investment. However, they can represent good value for money if they help you into a role you want more easily or quickly than would otherwise have happened.

If you decide that a career coach is what you need, then choosing the right coach/coaching company is important. Here are some guidelines on what to look for:

- specialist training and experience in career coaching and working with individuals in career transition
- membership of an appropriate professional body following a code of practice, such as the Career Development Institute
- evidence of continuous updating of their knowledge, including the coach receiving regular supervision with a trained coaching supervisor
- expectations are clear, open and transparent, and there is a written contract that reflects this understanding and outlines all fees, obligations, etc.
- the company's and the coach's reputation, and that you feel comfortable and safe working with them both – trust your instincts on this one.

IN A NUTSHELL

- Other people are a fantastic resource: ask them for advice, feedback and support.
- Check out the free career information services available to help you.
- Commercial career services can be a very good investment if you choose wisely.

19 AND FINALLY…

As you have been reading this book, completing the activities and devising your CV, the intention has been that you have also acquired some of the essential skills of career management, that is:

- knowing what you have to offer an employer
- understanding your target market
- how to articulate the above to an employer in an authentic and compelling way.

This means that when you go to an interview and they ask, 'Why should we employ you?', you will genuinely know why.

It will also be of immense help to you when you are networking for your next role, looking for promotion or planning a future career change; in fact, throughout your career.

The truth is, in a competitive recruitment marketplace, it is not always those who are most capable who get the job – it is those who understand and apply those principles of career management.

If you would like some help with your career management, then take a look at my book Career Coach, or come and see us at Personal Career Management (**www.personalcareermanagement.com**) for career coaching and outplacement services. We would love to hear from you.

Wishing you every success!

Corinne Mills